THE STRUCTURE OF AIKIDO VOLUME 1

Kenjutsu and *Taijutsu*

Sword and Open-hand
Movement Relationships

By Gaku Homma
Translated by Emily Busch

Frog, Ltd.
Berkeley, California

Domo Productions
Denver, Colorado

The Structure of Aikido, Volume 1
Kenjutsu and Taijutsu—Sword and Open-hand Movement Relationships

Published by Frog, Ltd.
and Domo Productions/Nippon Kan
   1365 Osage Street
   Denver, Colorado 80204

Frog, Ltd. books are distributed by
North Atlantic Books
P.O. Box 12327
Berkeley, California 94712

Cover art by Andrea DuFlon, Matt Meeks
Cover photography by Bryon Hays
Book design and illustrations by Gaku Homma
Photographs by Art Kaufmann

Printed in the United States of America by Malloy Lithographing

Library of Congress Cataloging-in-Publication Data

Homma, Gaku, 1950-
    The structure of aikido / by Gaku Homma; translated by Emily Busch
      p.   cm.
    Contents: v. 1. Kenjutsu and taijutsu, sword and open-hand movement relationships.
      ISBN 1-883319-55-2 (v. 1: pbk.)
      1. Aikido. 2. Kendo. 3. Hand-to-hand fighting, Oriental.

I. Title.
GV1114.35.H667   1997
796.8'154—dc20   96-36202

Table of Contents

Foreword

This book, Volume 1 in a three-volume series entitled *The Structure of Aikido* focuses on the relationship between *kenjutsu*—sword movement—and Aikido *taijutsu*—open-hand movement. Volume 2 in this series focuses on the relationship between *jojutsu*—staff movement—and Aikido *taijutsu* movement. Volume 3 provides training methods and exercises for developing skills in basic *ken* (sword) and *jo* (staff) movement. Usually the most basic training methods are found in the introductory chapters of the first volume, but I have saved them for the third volume for a particular reason. I feel it is important to have a broader understanding of how the movements generally apply to open-hand techniques before concentrating on repetitive base-movement exercises. My approach has been first to explore the movements as they flow together to form techniques both with a *ken* and open-handed before focusing on rote training methods. Approaching training in this manner helps to avoid becoming locked into patterns of stiff mechanical movement.

Engaging in years of study in the history and origins of Aikido as well as other martial arts, I have trained diligently in order to develop the *kenjutsu* and *jojutsu* to *taijutsu* relationship system depicted in these volumes. Since I first came to the United States in 1976, it has been an underlying goal of mine to develop a method for unifying these three forms of movement. The teaching method published in these volumes is what has become Aikido Nippon Kan's original practice method.

In 1984 I produced a *kenjutsu* and *taijutsu* relationship video series. This three-part series was the first of its kind to my knowledge to be produced in the United States or Japan. Originally created for my students to study at home, the series was filmed with home video equipment of that era's vintage. Subsequently, as the series was distributed throughout the US, even the original master tapes became worn and could not be used again for reproduction. Distribution had to be discontinued. In response to the requests I have had since that time, I have researched and developed the material for this book series.

When I first came to the United States, in the *dojos* I visited there were very few if any training weapons *(bokken* or wooden practice sword and *jo* or wooden staff). Occasionally I found *dojos* that displayed racks of *bokken* and *jo* on their walls as a show of martial spirit, but they were for decoration only. At the time, there were no Japanese instructors that I am aware of who taught *kenjutsu* and *jojutsu* movement as it relates to Aikido *taijutsu* movement. The weapons training I did see was limited to *suburi* (exercises using *ken* and *jo* for developing basic technique), or weapons training was taught independently from Aikido as in Iaido (the art of drawing one's sword, cutting an opponent, and sheathing the sword, all in one motion).

In some *dojos,* weapons training or practice with the *ken* and *jo* is still limited to black belt-level students. Less advanced and beginning students are discouraged or sometimes even excluded from practice with these weapons. At my *dojo* while teaching a class one day, I asked all of my students to please get their *ken* and *jo* for practice. I was surprised to see one visiting student run to the corner and kneel in *seiza* (formal kneeling position) as the others retrieved their weapons. When I asked him why, he informed me that white belt students at his *dojo* were not allowed to practice with weapons. At Nippon Kan, learning *kenjutsu* and *jojutsu* and their movement relationship to open-hand Aikido movement is a basic and important training for students of all levels—especially beginning students. This training is just as important as learning basic *ukemi* (the art of falling) such as front and back rolls.

The weapon relationships explored in this series are different from the weapons training originally practiced in the United States. This is a relatively new field of study, and I find the recent trend for instructors and students, especially American instructors and students, to be studying the relationship of weapons to open-hand movement to be a positive one. The founder of Aikido, Morihei Ueshiba, taught us that the practice of Aikido must be allowed to change and develop multidimensionally. The practice of Aikido is not stagnant but should develop day by day, transforming naturally. For this reason, I am proud to be able to share my Aikido practice method with you.

For beginning students, I hope this series will help to demonstrate the relationship between *kenjutsu, jojutsu,* and Aikido open-hand movement. For advanced students and instructors, I hope this book will add to your resources as we develop this new field of study.

My practice of Aikido still continues, and my understanding of Aikido movement and philosophy continues to change. As a result, this series is not an ending, and it will at some point most likely require a later edition to include new developments and discoveries.

For this three-volume series, 6,000 photos were selected from 12,000 negatives. It was my wish to use even more photographs to illustrate the movement more smoothly, but this proved impractical. Instead I have used text to help illustrate the relationships as clearly as possible.

The photographer for this project, Reverend Arthur Kauffman, is a student of mine who has been deeply involved in the founding and subsequent growth of Aikido Nippon Kan. Emily Busch, translator and editor of this and some of my past works, has taken much time away from her career as a jewelry designer to devote countless hours to the completion of this series. John Cruise, who has also served as editor on previous works, helped greatly in the production of this series. With the help of the above-mentioned people, Nippon Kan staff and members, and the publishing staff of North Atlantic Books and Frog Ltd., this series has become a reality. Many thanks to everyone.

Gaku Homma

Denver, January 1997

Some of the defensive techniques depicted in this book can cause serious injury. It is advised that great caution be taken in their practice and execution. The author and publisher hereby disclaim any and all responsibility or liability for injury that may occur as a result of the use or misuse of this material.

Chapter 1
Introduction

Volume 1 in this three-volume series focuses on manners, etiquette, *ukemi* (the art of falling), as well as basic body movement. This book's study of basic body movement is defined by the basic movements performed with the *ken* (sword) and their direct relationship to *taijutsu* (open hand) movement. *Ken* movement is broken down initially into two sections, *shinogi* or the preliminary movement engaged in before the actual techniques, and *sabaki* or the actual finish to the techniques themselves.

More than 1,600 photos have been used to illustrate more than sixty Aikido techniques. The photos and text are organized to show a clear relationship, motion for motion, between *kenjutsu*, *tateki no kurai* (multiple attackers), and *taijutsu* movement. Much care has been taken to match each movement in each category, but timing the shutter speeds for each sequence proved to be extremely difficult, and in a few cases the movement may vary by a frame or two. In these cases if you examine the previous and subsequent frame to one in question you should be able to pick up the relationships clearly.

One might expect to find a history of Aikido in the introduction of a book about the practice of Aikido. Even if we were to focus on the history of Aikido in Japan alone, this would be a monumental task. Today in Japan there are countless Aikido organizations and more headquarters than there are fingers on my hands. Each claim a place in Aikido's history. This, combined with the activity over the last few decades in the United States, Europe, indeed all over the world, makes for enough material to fill volumes. In an effort to be fair, and also so that this book may be beneficial to Aikido students of any political or historical background, I chose simply to leave the subject of history for another book, another time.

Is it relevant to us now who invented the first computer? Or who invented the first game of football? Even though we may not know the answers to these questions we can still use computers to enhance our lives, or watch a game of football to entertain ourselves. I think this holds true for the practice of Aikido as well. What is important is the joy and understanding we gain from practice itself. The beginning Aikidoist practices just for the sake of practice, and it is this purity that gives us unlimited freedom for the future development of the martial arts. We all should admire and respect the great leaders of history, but at the same time we must realize that we are also individuals. It is not necessary to wear the robes of the leaders of our past, or try to hang onto them. A important part of martial art training, I believe, is not to lose sight of self-development and self-discovery. This pursuit can become distorted or lost.

If you need this information there are many books on the history of Aikido available. I would make two suggestions. First, make sure you read a number of sources to gain a wide perspective. I also suggest that you read about the history of Japan as a whole, including its sociology, religion, arts, etc., to gain a more complete understanding of Aikido's historical background.

Chapter 2
Reiho
Practice Etiquette and How to Handle the *Ken*

Reiho—Practice Etiquette

There are a few basic rules of etiquette for handling the *ken*. *Ken* is the Japanese word for a steel-bladed sword. During practice and in this series, a *bokken* (wooden sword) is commonly used. *Boku* is the Japanese word for wood, and *ken* is the Japanese word for sword. Sometimes the wooden sword is called a *bokuto*. *Boku* again translates as wood, and *to* is another word for sword. Although we will be using *bokken* in this series, the rules and etiquette depicted here are those for the use of the *ken* or steel-bladed sword. In traditional Japanese schools of swordsmanship, the rules of etiquette and even the techniques and stances vary from school to school, and each style has its own interpretation. At times, a particular school might adopt a certain stance or a strange pose or technique solely to differentiate it from other schools. This book presents a culmination of the most widely accepted rules of manners and etiquette associated with the sword.

Practice etiquette is called *reiho*. The purpose of *reiho* is deeper than simply bowing to the front shrine of a *dojo*. There are specific reasons why we are concerned with the careful handling of a *ken* during practice. The most important reason is to create and maintain a mind-set of concentration and undistracted thinking. Focusing on respect for a *ken* before, during, and after practice helps to prevent accidents. I have watched students respectfully bow to the front shrine with their *ken* before practice, and to their partners before they begin to work together, because these manners have been taught to them. Unfortunately, during practice, I have also seen them lean on their *ken* as if it were a golf club, or carry it over their shoulder like a baseball bat. In these instances it is clear that such students are aware of the physical ritual of bowing, but they do not deeply understand that the attitude behind these movements is one of respect, concentration, and a consideration for safety.

On a certain level it is difficult to explain why and how someone affords such respect for a stick of wood. That is a subject that is very difficult to teach, and may be something that needs to be reflected upon in the perimeters of your own expectations. At my *dojo*, *reiho* signals a beginning and an end to a safe practice.

Reiho Seiza Rei (Kneeling Bow) to the Front Shrine

From *seiza* (kneeling position), begin by placing the *ken* about one foot in front of you horizontally. The *tsuka* or hilt is to the left, cutting edge of the blade facing toward you. As you sit in *seiza*, your right big toe should cross slightly over your left big toe behind you. In Japan, during *Shinto* ceremonies, women traditionally place their left toe over their right. In reality it is not absolutely critical which toe is crossed on top of the other, but traditionally it is right over left for *seiza rei*. What is important is that you do not cross the bridges of your feet beneath you. Sit with your back straight, knees slightly apart, about the width of three fists. (Traditionally the space between the knees for women is two fists.) Both hands should rest lightly on the front of your thighs.

To bow properly from *seiza*, place your left hand palm down on the mat in front of you. Then place your right hand down, with your index fingers and thumbs touching each other slightly. Your hands should form a triangular space between them. With a straight back bow forward until your nose is centered over the triangular space your hands have created. Your eyes should be cast downward toward the mat. This type of bow is reserved for bowing to the front shrine, and should not be used when bowing to a partner. Because this is a bow of deep respect, your eyes are cast downward. Interestingly, the triangular space formed between your hands offers protection for your nose should your head be pushed forward forcefully to the mat from behind. Also for your protection, it is important that you do not place all of your body weight over your hands when you bow forward. Having more of your weight over your center allows you to shift your position quickly.

Ritsu Rei (Standing Bow) to the Front Shrine

Stand with your feet slightly apart yet parallel. Place your *ken* in both hands, *tsuka* to the left, cutting edge of the blade toward you. Raise the *ken* up with both hands to about eye level. Bow your head and upper torso slightly, eyes cast downward toward the mat.

Seiza Rei (Kneeling Bow) with a Partner

Bowing to a partner from *seiza* is the same as bowing to the front shrine with a few exceptions. When bowing to a partner, your *ken* is placed on your left side slightly behind you with the *tsuka gashira* (bottom end of the hilt normally held by the pinkie finger of your left hand) even with, or slightly behind, your left shoulder. The cutting edge of the blade should be toward you. Traditionally, the reason for this display of etiquette was to demonstrate to your partner your lack of intention to attack. This is attained by placing the *ken* in a position that is not readily available for immediate use. When you bow to your partner, the angle of your bow is not as deep as for the front shrine, bowing to approximately a forty-five-degree angle. While bowing your head forward slightly, keep your eyes cast forward, paying attention to your partner's movements. To keep both partners in the frame for the photo shown, both partners are quite close together. In actuality, there should be about eight to ten feet between you. This is also true for *ritsu rei* with a partner during practice. *Seiza rei* with a partner is performed after *seiza rei* to the front shrine.

Ritsu Rei (Standing Bow) with a Partner

Stand facing your partner with the *ken* held in your left hand, cutting edge of the blade facing upward, *tsuka* forward. Hold the *ken* by balancing it about one-third of the distance from the *tsuka gashira* toward the middle. Bow your upper torso and head forward to about a thirty-degree angle. Your eyes should be cast forward, about level with your partner's knees, paying attention to his or her movements.

Above: Seiza Rei (kneeling bow to the front shrine).

Right: Ritsu Rei (standing bow to the front shrine).

Above: Seiza Rei (kneeling bow with a partner).

Right: Ritsu Rei (standing bow with a partner).

How to Handle the *Ken*

As a way to signal the beginning and end of practice, we bow to the shrine at the front of the *dojo*. There are also specific ways to handle your *ken* before and after practice that signal your intentions through your actions. There is specific etiquette for retrieving your *ken* from the racks in the *dojo*, replacing it, and carrying your *ken* to and from practice.

Top photos: Holding the *ken* before and after practice.

In your right hand, with the cutting edge of the blade facing upward, the *kissaki* (the first few inches of the blade near the tip used for cutting) is pointed forward, the *tsuka* (hilt) to the rear. In the days of the samurai, *ken* were carried in a case on the left side, so they could be drawn quickly with the right hand. Holding your *ken* in your right hand with the cutting edge of the blade facing upward signals a non-aggressive posture. It is considered respectful and polite. This is also true for carrying a rifle when not in use.

Middle photos: Holding the *ken* during practice while not engaged but in a ready position.

Hold the *ken* in your left hand with the cutting edge of the blade facing upward. Your *tsuka* is pointed forward, with your *kissaki* to the rear. From this stance, your *ken* can be drawn readily to engage in practice. If you were carrying a steel-bladed sword, it would still be sheathed in its case in this position.

Bottom photos: Holding the *ken* during practice in a rest position.

Hold the *ken* with both hands, right hand forward with your *kissaki* lowered to the rear, behind you to your right. This stance is assumed when practice has been interrupted temporarily, for example, when pausing to receive instruction.

Ken no Kamae (Stance with the sword)

There is an old saying in Japan that the only specific *kamae* (stance or posture) used with the *ken* is no specific stance at all. There are many postures and variations of postures which can be assumed. The most generally accepted stance used when facing a partner to begin practice is called *seigan no kamae*. From this stance many other *kamae* can be readily assumed. *Seigan* is the Japanese word depicting a point on your head right between the eyes. As you assume *seigan no kamae*, your *ken* should be pointed directly at that spot right between your partner's eyes. As illustrated in the top right photo, if your partner assumes this stance correctly you cannot tell the length of his *ken*.

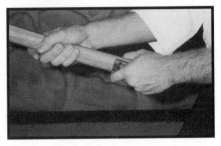

Above: Correct kamae.

To hold the *ken* correctly, relax. The grip with your hands is not rigid. Grip with your index fingers loosely, and the pinkie fingers on both hands held more tightly—as if you were wringing out a towel. With both arms relaxed, try not to lean backward with your weight over your heels. Extend your attention forward. Imagine that you are standing lightly on newly formed ice on a winter morning, relaxed but ready to move in a split second. The feeling should be like that of a cat ready to pounce on a mouse.

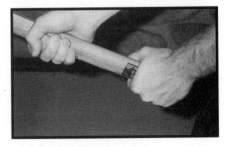

Above: Incorrect kamae.

Chapter 3
Basic Body Movement

At the same time you push open a door, you naturally take a step forward or you will lose your balance. To pull a door open you naturally take a step backward, or as a consequence the door will hit you in the face. If someone were to push you from behind, your instinctive reaction would be to step forward so as not to fall. These natural reactions also are a very important part of basic *ken* movement.

Dealing effectively with the actions of an opponent does not depend on special techniques or exotic poses or postures. Unlike some martial arts that adopt the movements of animals, we do not do this in Aikido. It is not necessary for us to mimic the actions of monkeys and cranes, or even mythical beings such as dragons, to practice Aikido. It has taken considerable effort for us to evolve into human beings, and we need to make the most of this human opportunity.

Our most effective movements are those we do naturally, automatically. If you take a step with your left foot, the next step you take normally is with your right. Simple movements like these that we use every day are the most powerful and effective movements we have available to us.

Your own natural movements are not something you learn from a martial art school, or even something you learned from your parents. This sense and ability you have developed yourself since birth. We can apply these movements readily when we are working with the *ken* or when we are practicing Aikido open-handed because our bodies already know them instinctively.

Your mind controls your body's movements or performance. Your body's movements and performance also control your mind. The influence your body and your mind have on each other is not one-directional. If you are now thirty years old and began to walk at the age of one year, you already have been training for twenty-nine years in your own style of movement. Even if you were to train daily in the martial arts for ten years, it would not be comparable to the twenty-nine years of training in your own style of natural movement you have already had. It is important for us to incorporate these "twenty-nine" years of experience in our practice of the martial arts. As we practice Aikido, we develop and refine these movements that are already so ingrained in us naturally. This seems to me to be a rational and sensible path to follow. It would not be incorrect to say that a person thirty years of age has already had twenty-nine years of experience practicing Aikido.

In Aikido *taijutsu* the footwork is made up primarily of three basic movements, not including stepping forward and stepping backward. These three simple movements we all use on a daily basis to keep ourselves safe from harm. You are able to read this book right now because all day you used your own natural movements to protect yourself. How many times did you hit a door today? Or run into a wall? Or bump into someone? If you had not been using your own natural movements to protect yourself, you would either be lying in a hospital bed by now, or in a tight-fitting box decorated with wreaths of flowers! These movements, along with the attitude of conflict resolution that begets them, help to deal with conflict. I teach this concept of "conflict resolution movement" as part of our official beginner's class curriculum.

These basic movements are not only useful when coming in contact with human beings; they are just as useful to help you get around a telephone pole in your path, or avoid a child on a bicycle coming toward you. The concept of these movements does not apply only to actual physical situations such as working with a partner practicing Aikido, but to other types of relationships in our lives on an emotional and intellectual level. The concept of these movements applies to relationships of all kinds: business, family, or friends, for example.

Three Basic Movements: Triangle △, Circle ○, Square □

Let's take a closer look at what these three basic movements are.

Imagine that you are walking forward in a straight line, and someone is walking toward you from the other direction, directly in your path. If you both continue to walk toward each other on this same path you will eventually collide. In this situation we have three primary options open to us.

• As someone approaches you, open to the side as illustrated in figure 1.

• As someone approaches you, *tenkan* (spin) as illustrated in figure 2 & 3.

• As someone approaches you, step out to the side and then back in as illustrated in figure 4.

These three simple movements make up the foundation for all of the techniques we use when we practice Aikido open-handed. They also make up the basic movements we use when we practice *kenjutsu*. As I will explain in the following chapters, *kenjutsu* movement is divided into two major categories, *shinogi* and *sabaki*. All *kenjutsu shinogi* and *sabaki* movements are made of these three movements as well.

The movement illustrated in figure 1, if executed symmetrically to the left and right side, forms a triangular pattern. The movement illustrated in figures 2 and 3, if executed on both sides, forms a pattern in the shape of a circle. Subsequently the movement illustrated in figure 4, executed on both sides, forms a square. Therefore our basic body movement can be represented by these three symbols, △ ○ □. We can connect these three movements in an endless variety of combinations that forms the base for all of our Aikido techniques.

As a reference in the following chapters, a triangle △ will symbolize an opening movement (figure 1). A circle ○ will symbolize a *tenkan* or spinning movement (figures 2 and 3), and a square □ will symbolize a zigzag movement (figure 4).

To begin exploring these three movements, have your partner strike *shomen uchi* (frontal strike) toward you with a *ken*. First practice all three movements △ ○ □ statically, one at a time. As you become familiar with each movement individually, have your partner strike *shomen uchi* more freely in succession, and use all three movements to avoid your partner's strikes. At first you can practice this exercise without holding a *ken* in your hands as you concentrate on your footwork.

This is very important basic training for developing a sense for two different types of movement: *irimi* (entering in toward your partner) and *tenkan* (a spinning motion to the outside behind, or to the inside in front of your partner).

BASIC BODY MOVEMENT 11

△ Symbolizes *hiraki* (opening) movement

Hiraki foot movement (figure 1)

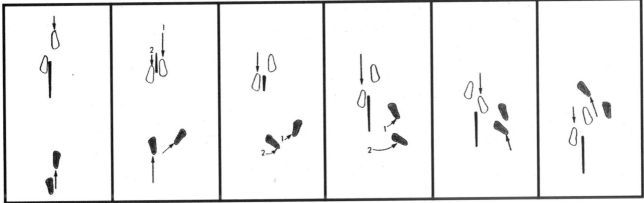

Face to face with your partner, right foot forward.	*As your partner swings up, step to the right with your right foot.*	*As your partner strikes downward …*	*Open by stepping to the right with your left foot behind your right foot.*	*Having completed this hiraki (opening) movement …*	*Step in behind your partner at an angle with your left foot.*

Top photos: Ken versus open-hand hiraki movement

Bottom photos: Both-elbow grab—Timing throw. Open-hand hiraki movement

○ Symbolizes *tenkan* (spinning) movement

To the outside is *soto tenkan*; to the inside is *uchi tenkan*.

Soto tenkan foot movement (figure 2)

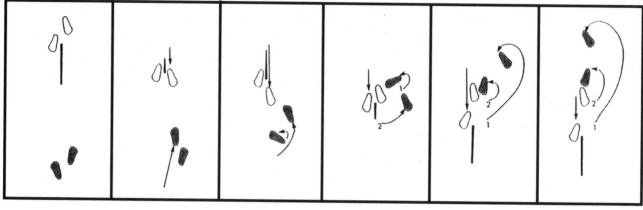

As your partner swings up to strike, slide in left foot forward.

As he reaches the top of his strike, step in right foot forward.

Pivot on your right foot …

… as you bring your left foot back and spin to the outside.

Your new position is slightly behind your partner facing the same direction.

Uchi tenkan foot movement (figure 3)

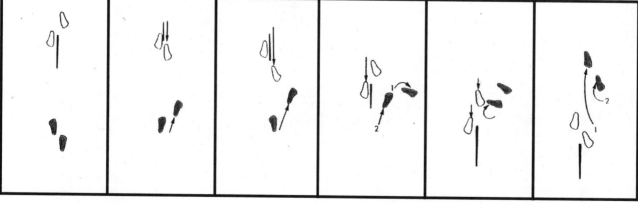

Face to face with your partner, left foot forward.

As your partner swings up to strike, slide in right foot forward to the right.

As he reaches the top of his strike …

… step in to the right with your left foot and pivot.

Bring your right foot back as you spin to the inside.

Your new position is slightly behind your partner facing the same direction.

Top photos: Ken versus open hand; soto tenkan movement (to the outside). Bottom photos: Punch—Wrist twist; open-hand soto tenkan movement (to the outside)

Top photos: Ken versus open hand; uchi tenkan movement (to the inside). Bottom photos: Opposite hand grab— Rolling throw; open-hand uchi tenkan movement (to the inside)

☐ Symbolizes *irimi* (entering) movement

Irimi foot movement (figure 4)

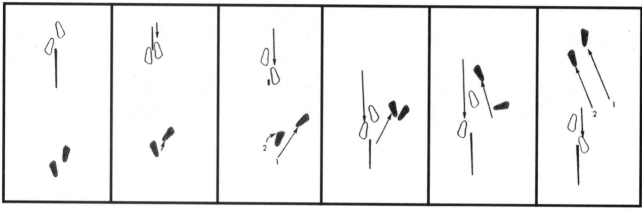

Face to face with your partner, right foot forward.	*As your partner strikes, slide forward and to the right.*	*As he strikes downward …*	*… angle in behind him …*	*… stepping forward to the left and behind your partner.*	*This is a zigzag foot movement.*

Top photos: Ken versus open hand; irimi movement. Bottom photos: Both-hands grab—Sky and ground throw; open-hand irimi movement

When practicing these movements, it is important to remember that these are movements you use every day. It is not necessary to position yourself in unnaturally wide stances, or to worry too much about precise angles your feet are supposed to be positioned in. If you limit the scope or range of your movement, you compromise your own flexibility. Practicing limited, tightly defined movement tends to result in a loss of agility. From a tactical point of view, training in a "cookie-cutter fashion" can put you at a disadvantage, because if an opponent were to force you beyond the limits of your repertoire, you would easily be defeated. As a means of resolving conflict with a positive outcome, we use relaxed natural movement instead.

Above all, the concept behind these three movements is a simple one. Instead of trying to block an on-coming strike, it is better to first move out of the way. By letting go of your initial position, the opportunity to move into a technique presents itself. The oncoming strike from a partner gives you the opportunity to utilize your movements to "share, care, and give way" in a fashion that results in being "fair" to both yourself and your partner. You first give away one position to regain your objective from a new vantage point. This is the mind-set of conflict resolution at the core of Aikido. Why? Another simple answer. If you do not get out of the way, the results are painful. It hurts to be on the receiving end of an oncoming strike! By giving up your first position, the path is a much smoother one to follow. In this sense, we can say that the way of Aikido is one of peace.

Think about techniques that you know and try to break them down in your mind into the three basic foot-body movements, △ ○ □. I have illustrated three examples on the following pages to help with this exercise. If you study these figures you should begin to discover that these three movements combine to form the structure of all of our techniques. In recent years it seems to have been a popular trend in the United States for Aikido movement to be flowing and loosely defined. Although this has its merits, if you study the movement of the founder of Aikido, Morihei Ueshiba, you can find these three shapes as distinctly as if they had been drawn onto the mat.

All three movements—△ ○ □—illustrated in open-hand techniques

Frontal strike—Entering throw △ ○ □ movement.

Frontal strike   *△ hiraki (opening) movement*   *○ soto tenkan (spin to the outside) movement*   *□ irimi (entering) zigzag movement*

Side strike—Four-direction throw △ ○ □ movement.

Side strike   *△ hiraki (opening) movement*   *○ uchi tenkan (spin to the inside) movement*   *□ irimi (entering) movement*

Behind-both-wrists grab—Wrist twist △ ○ ○ □

Partner grabs your left hand with his left hand   △ *hiraki (opening) movement*   ○ *uchi tenkan (spin to the inside) movement*   *Grab over your partner's wrist …*

… ○ soto tenkan (spin to the outside) movement   □ *irimi (entering) movement*

Although the interpretation and application of the triangle, circle, and square portrayed in this series is my own, the concept of the triangle, circle, and square is not new in association with Aikido. For example, I have seen in Aikido publications articles on *ikumusubi, tarumusubi,* and *tamatsunemusubi* but only as they relate in a spiritual or religious context to Shintoism and Zen Buddhism.

These spiritual explanations and ideologies are difficult for most of us to understand. It is an illusion, I believe, to think that being able to understand these religious concepts intellectually is the same as truly understanding them. The triangle, circle, and square may make a popular t-shirt design, but there is a difference between admiring a design and understanding its true spiritual meaning. It is comprehensible that a martial artist over the age of eighty, as the founder was, would turn to the spiritual and religious realms in his later teachings.

Personally, at my present age, my own path of practice and my interpretation and application of these symbols needs to be more realistic and useful. I need to start on a more basic, down-to-earth level, concentrating first on how these symbols relate to my own physical body movement. This has been my inspiration.

The symbols are not peculiar to Aikido. If we go back through history, the triangle, circle, and square have been prevalent symbols for centuries. In the study of Zen or Esoteric Buddhism, these symbols have been used for more than 1,300 years. Interestingly enough, these symbols have also been associated with the arts of war. In records dating back 350 years, these symbols can be found to depict certain battlefield strategies employed with armies numbering in the thousands.

For example: (1) When approached by a large army, a defending army would open its ranks to let an enemy formation enter, only to close in and attack from behind. This strategy is symbolized by the triangle. (2) As an approaching army attacked from the front, two smaller groups of defenders would deflect and steer the approaching leaders into circles to the sides, where they could be neutralized. This strategy is symbolized by the circle. (3) As an army approached, a strategy for the defending army was first to engage the enemy head on, then dash to the side and back to their rear. As they tried to regroup, the enemy could then be assaulted from behind. This strategy is symbolized by the square. Also chronicled in these military records is the saying that a good swordsman is also a good strategist.

Throughout human history, and in our daily movement today, we find the triangle, circle, and square. These movements give us balance in our life, and form the basis for our body-foot movement in both Aikido and *kenjutsu*. Where do our arm movements come from in Aikido? If you look carefully at *kenjutsu* movement, you can find the answer to that question.

Chapter 4
Kihon Ken No Sosaho
Basic Sword Movement

This chapter focuses on how to deal effectively with the movement of an oncoming partner with a *ken*. We will explore how to initiate or receive and counter the advances of a partner with a *ken* by focusing on *shinogi* and *sabaki* movement.

Even if you have been practicing Aikido for a long time, most likely this is the first time you have encountered these two terms. Let's start with some definitions. If you look up the word *shinogi* in a Japanese/English dictionary, the first definition of *shinogi* is the ridge-line on both sides of a sword blade. *Shinogi* also by definition means to endure, or to have patience, or to bear. The third definition in the dictionary is to defend, or to survive bad times.

The ridge-line of a sword is called the *shinogi*, and so is the ridge-line of a *bokken*. If you repeatedly use a *bokken* to strike an opposing *bokken* in *kumitachi (bokken* to *bokken* practice), you will eventually wear down this ridge-line and the *bokken* will take on an oval appearance. After much use, if a *bokken* shows dents and signs of wear on the cutting edge, but the *shinogi* line is crisp and free of dents, the *bokken* has not been used properly in practice.

In response to an attack by a partner with a *bokken*, the *shinogi* is used by the receiving partner to field the attack. It is not used to directly block an oncoming strike with force. If you use your *bokken* for this purpose, you will break your weapon. We have had hundreds of students at seminars, and the majority of students who break their weapons are beginners. The correct use of the *bokken* when fielding an oncoming strike is to utilize a little cushion in your movements, using your *bokken* to absorb the shock of the oncoming blow instead of trying to block it directly. In Japanese we use the expression *"shinogi o kezuru"* which means to "peel the *shinogi*." This translates when using your *bokken* to moving so that your *bokken* glances off your partner's oncoming strike. "Peeling a shaving" off the *shinogi* of your partner's *bokken* instead of meeting it straight on. A useful analogy might be that of striking flint to make a spark for fire. You do not strike the pieces together directly, but have them glance off one another at an oblique angle. It is this flint-striking or peeling motion that is used to field a strike. Still today in Japan, the phrase *shinogi o kezuru* is used to describe an evenly matched game or fiercely fought close contest.

The word *sabaki* is defined in the dictionary as the judgments passed by a judge in a court of law. It is subsequently defined as the effective management of a situation, and the skillful use of intricate tools and materials. The last definition given is to clean and de-bone a fish, and interestingly, the word *sabaki* is used as a slang term for murder.

In applying these two terms to the use of the *ken,* a partner's *shodachi* (initial strike) is fielded or managed with *shinogi* movement, and subsequent strikes are countered and resolved with *sabaki* movement. The structure of all of the techniques we practice in Aikido is made up of these two distinct types of movement: *shinogi* and *sabaki.* All five *ken shinogi* and all seven *ken sabaki* movements illustrated in this volume are made up of △ ○ □ movements.

Shinogi

Most people have played handball or racquetball, or have at least watched it being played. To return a ball successfully that has been played off a wall in these games requires a lot of skill. It requires a great deal of control of wrist and arm movements as well as total body coordination for both balance and power. In the way that players return balls straight forward, or use the floor and side walls, I see a great similarity to *kenjutsu* movement. Like responding to a rebounding ball, dealing with the advance of a partner's strike in *kenjutsu* is what is important. Another important skill in both racquet sports and *kenjutsu* is being able to anticipate movement before it happens. In racquetball, it is vital to be able to discern where a ball will bounce before it even hits the wall, and to respond accordingly. This same sense is needed in *kenjutsu*. In tennis, for example, strategy is used to force your partner to come to the net to return a shallow ball, leaving him out of position for a deep back court slam. This same kind of strategy is also evident in *kenjutsu*.

In *kenjutsu*, if a partner is to strike, he or she must be 100 percent committed to their actions. If there is any doubt or hesitation in their minds they will either be unable to attack, or will by their lack of commitment open themselves up to a counter-attack. For their advance to be effective, there must be complete coordination of mind and body. To deal with the tremendous power that is generated by the strike or thrust of a committed partner and turn it to your advantage is the purpose of *shinogi* movement. To receive a blow directly can have adverse effects if your partner is more powerful than you are. Instead of trying to match pound for pound the strength inherent in an initial attack, it makes more sense to diffuse this energy by dodging the first blow. *Shinogi* movement accomplishes this directive, and also moves you to a new position that is not only safe, but a strategic position from which to counter-strike.

If your partner delivers an initial strike with serious commitment and misses, he or she must follow up with an additional attack. It is this moment, when your partner tries to adjust and follow with an additional attack, that you seize upon to counter-attack. This is when *sabaki* movement is used. A Japanese poem illustrates this concept: *In a sudden downpour, open your umbrella under the sanctuary of the eaves.*

As a sudden shower begins, it is best to first find a dry sanctuary under the protection of the eaves of a roof before opening your umbrella to deal with the rain. The rain in this case symbolizes the attack of an enemy. Stepping under the protection of the eaves is *shinogi* movement, and opening the umbrella is *sabaki* movement.

In handball, racquetball, tennis, and baseball, each sport has its own techniques for dealing with oncoming balls. When working with the *ken* we also have particular techniques we use. Because the range of motion of an initial attack varies widely, the *shinogi* and *sabaki* movements we use also have a wide range of flexibility in their applications. In this section we explore five *shinogi* movements that relate to popular, basic, open-hand Aikido techniques. These five *shinogi* can first be practiced without a partner, then with a partner, striking *shomen uchi* (frontal strike), *yokomen uchi* (side strike), and *tsuki* (thrusting cut) with a *ken*. Begin by having your partner strike static one strike at a time as you practice each different *shinogi* movement. When you become more familiar with each movement, have your partner strike repeatedly, and practice associating freely different strikes with different *shinogi* movements. All *shinogi* movements illustrated can be executed to either the right or the left side.

1. Awase shinogi △

Against *shomen uchi* or *yokomen uchi*.

As your partner swings up to strike *shomen uchi*, match his movements. As your partner cuts downward, open to the right with a glancing block over your partner's *ken*. Squeeze both hands together as you grip your *ken* to block. This kind of glancing blow is called *seka no atari* and refers to the glancing blow made when striking flint stones together to make a spark.

Practice Points

Once you have completed *awase shinogi*, remain erect with your *ken* trained on your partner in front of you. *Do not* bend forward incorrectly, with your eyes focused on the mat and your *ken* directed behind you, as shown in the photo to the right.

Incorrect ending posture

Kenjutsu

Taijutsu—open to the right

Taijutsu—open to the left

2. Uchi otoshi shinogi △

Against *tsuki*, *katamunedori*, *gyaku hanmi katatedori*, etc.

From a close distance, your partner *tsukis*, or you both remain deadlocked in *seigan kamai* (stance with your *ken* held in front of you directed at a point between your partner's eyes). Open to the right or the left, using the *shinogi* of your *ken* to block over your partner's *ken*, forcing it back behind him. (Similar to a net drop shot in tennis.)

When opening to the right, your right hand is palm down over your ken, completely extended toward the mat.

When opening to the left, your right hand is twisted palm up, yet extended downward after you have blocked over your partner's ken.

Kenjutsu

Taijutsu—open to the right

Taijutsu—open to the left

3. Waki shinogi △

Against *shomen uchi, yokomen uchi, gyaku hanmi katatedori, ryotedori, ryokatadori, katadori,* all *ushiro* techniques, etc.

From a wide distance, as your partner swings up to strike, *tsuki* toward his face with the *kissaki* of your *ken* (the first few inches near the tip of the sword used for cutting) to distract him. As your partner strikes downward, open to the right or the left into *wakigamae* (a stance holding the sword at your side with the *kissaki* toward the rear).

In this opening move, you do not retreat straight backward. Matching your partner's speed, take one step to the side, then take one more step back with the other foot. As you move to the side, use your *kissaki* as a feint or check tactic to get your partner's attention. Like a magician that distracts you with one hand while performing a trick with the other, this feint provides you the opportunity to step off the line of his attack without attracting and re-directing his attention. Your field of vision should focus on your partner, not just his *ken*. Never open to the side so much that you show your back to your partner, or lean too far forward, tipping your shoulder. This *shinogi* can be used to move to the inside or the outside of your partner.

Kenjutsu

Taijutsu—open to the left

Taijutsu—open to the right

4. Kaburi shinogi △

Against *shomen uchi, gyaku hanmi* or *ai hanmi katatedori, ryotedori,* etc.

From a wide distance, your partner swings up to strike, or advances with a high *tsuki.* Move out to your left, raising your arms above your head, elbows bent, cutting up with your *ken.* As you finish this *shinogi* movement, your body position is low, with your *kissaki* trained on your partner.

Kaburi shinogi is not initiated until your partner has committed to his strike. As he swings up, first direct your *kissaki* toward his face as a feint to distract him. As he strikes downward, move out to the left, both arms raised. Follow with one more step in front, to cover. If your partner realizes which way you are moving, he will adjust his strike accordingly. Therefore, the feint allows you valuable time to move out of the way. *Kaburi shinogi* is not meant to directly block your partner's strike. The position of your *ken* provides protection from a glancing blow to the shoulder as you move out of range. It also moves you into position to make your next move. The feeling of *kaburi shinogi* is similar to skiing "bumps" or moguls. You use the moguls to spring from as you turn. *Kaburi shinogi* can be done to either the right or the left side.

Kenjutsu

Taijutsu—open to the left

Taijutsu—open to the left

5. Sumi shinogi △

Against *yokomen uchi, tsuki, gyaku hanmi katatedori, ryotedori, katatedori ryotemochi*, etc.

As your partner strikes *yokomen uchi*, low toward your lower leg, slide or step in to block. Whether you slide or step depends on whether the leg being targeted for the strike remains behind or moves forward.

Kenjutsu

Taijutsu—open to the right

Practice Points

Ma Ai	The distance between yourself and your partner.
Tou Ma	The total distance between you and your partner's front foot is the length of both your *kens* combined plus one half that distance. This term applies to *kenjutsu*. For *taijutsu* it describes the distance for wide-distance approaches.
Gobu	Also called *isoku itto no ma ai*, this is the distance between yourself and your partner, where if either of you were to take only one step, the *kissaki* of both swords would touch. This term applies to *kenjutsu*. For *taijutsu* it describes closer-distance approaches most commonly encountered during practice.
Chikama	As it applies to *kenjutsu*, the distance between you and your partner when you are able to cross your *ken* with each other's, locking them together about six inches from the *kissaki*. For *taijutsu* this distance is inherent in resistance or static techniques.
Tamoto	If your partner is in *migi hanmi* (right stance), the space to his right is called *tamoto*. *Tamoto* translates literally to mean "sleeve." In this series we refer to this side as your partner's back or outside.
Futokoro	If your partner is in *migi hanmi*, the space to his left is called *futokoro*, which translates as "the inside of a jacket." In this series we refer to this side as your partner's front or inside.

Sabaki

Now that we have introduced the five basic *shinogi* movements, let's take a look at basic *sabaki* movement. One of the jobs the postmaster must perform at the post office is sorting the mail into different slots before delivery. In Japanese, this kind of action is called *sabaki*. A card dealer proficient in shuffling and dealing cards is said to have skillful *sabaki*. If a chef is skillful as he scales and cleans a fish, it is said that he shows skillful *sabaki* with a knife.

It has already been described in this chapter how to use *shinogi* movement to avoid an initial strike from your partner. The purpose of *shinogi* movement is also to move you into a position from where you can move quickly into your own counter-strike, taking aim where your partner is vulnerable. If your *shinogi* movement is not done correctly, it is difficult to perform effective consecutive *sabaki* movement.

In *kenjutsu*, *shinogi* movement followed by *sabaki* movement is called *ato no sen*. To go directly into a *sabaki* movement without first performing a *shinogi* movement is called *sen no sen*. In *taijutsu*, you have the equivalent variations of movement, depending on if you do an opening move before you do a technique, or go directly into a technique without an opening move.

One exercise for practicing *sabaki* movement utilizes breath control. Using your voice, exhale slowly. See if you can swing up and strike thirty to forty times during that one exhalation. Make sure that you swing your *ken* fully up over your head each time. How to strengthen yourself and improve your skills at *sabaki* movement in solitary practice will be discussed in more detail in Volume 3. The *uchiuma* (hitting horse) and *tachiki* (trees or posts with protective barriers to absorb shock damage) are both excellent tools for this kind of practice.

To improve your skills at *shinogi* and *sabaki* movement together, it is useful to practice with the *tsurikiuchi* (hanging wood). Physically, this is a demanding workout, and to practice safely it is important to be alert at all times to others around you. For more information on safety for these practice techniques refer to Volume 3. In the reality of a serious attack by someone with a *ken*, there really are no rules or *kata* (forms or patterns used to learn movement) that must be followed. As part of our learning process, however, we need to break techniques down first into organized patterns that we can understand. This we will do with seven basic *sabaki* and their relationships to *taijutsu* movements. To practice the *sabaki* movement that is introduced in this chapter, try following these steps: 1) Work on the basic *sabaki* movements by yourself. This is called *suburi geiko* (repetitious exercises for developing basic technical movement with a *ken*). 2) Work with a partner. Have your partner strike *shomen uchi* as you practice the *sabaki* movements, slowly at first. 3) Have your partner alternate between *shomen uchi* and *tsuki*, as you add *shinogi* movements before the *sabaki* movements.

In the following pages, we will work with step three in more depth. Please compare carefully the *kenjutsu* and *taijutsu* photographs. The smaller photographs are *shinogi*, and the larger photographs are *sabaki* movements. The word *sassuru* in Japanese translates as "anticipate," or to catch the feeling of something as or before it happens. For example, a frontal strike can be described as a hit. Hit is spelled H-I-T. If you were to describe the action as it was being performed by the letters, the "H" would be the stance you were in as you began. The "I" would be the position you are in as your hand swings up over your head, and the "T" your downward strike. *Sassuru* applies to being able to anticipate action before the "H." If someone were to punch you, it would be spelled P-U-N-C-H. *Sassuru* means being able to anticipate this action before the "P." If you are calm and concentrate, it is easy to pick up on when and how your partner will move by slight movements in his eyes, shoulders, breathing, or a shifting of weight. Breathing is especially important. Just as a still pond can mirror its surroundings, we can too if we stay calm. We are also like the pond in the sense that if the surface is disturbed we no longer are able to see what is reflected around us. The point here is to keep calm.

1. *Omote kukuri otoshi sabaki*—Entering *kukuri otoshi sabaki* □

KENJUTSU

Example: against *tsuki* or *shomen uchi*.

As your partner *tsukis*
to your upper body …

… open to the right with
uchi otoshi shinogi.

As your partner
swings up again …

… slide forward and touch
your *kissaki* to his right wrist.

Enter with your whole body, cutting
forward on your partner's wrist.

Continue to slide, right foot forward in
front of him, using your *ken* to push him
forward, forcing his *ken* to the mat. Step
in with your left foot for a body block.

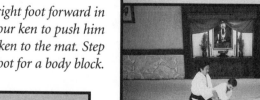

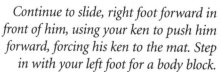

Practice Points

An older style would have you use your knee to strike *(atemi)* your
partner's ribs as you cut forward on his wrist. You can also use your
knee to knock your partner off balance once his *ken* has been forced to
the mat.

Ikkyo to *yonkyo omote*—Arm hold techniques (front)

TAIJUTSU

Example: against *tsuki, shomen uchi, gyaku hanmi katatedori,* etc.

Tsuki—Open to the right with uchi otoshi shinogi.

Shomen uchi—Open to the right with awase shinogi.

Gyaku hanmi katate-dori—Open to the right with waki shinogi.

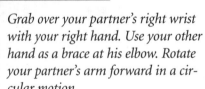

Grab over your partner's right wrist with your right hand. Use your other hand as a brace at his elbow. Rotate your partner's arm forward in a circular motion.

Slide in, right foot forward. If you step in with your left foot before your partner is under control, he can grab your leg as a counter.

Continue the circular motion until your palm is extended directly toward the mat above his elbow. Take one more step at an angle inward with your left foot, forcing your partner to the mat.

2. *Ushiro kukuri otoshi sabaki*—Turning *kukuri otoshi sabaki* ○

KENJUTSU
Example: against *shomen uchi.*

As your partner swings up to strike …

… slide in, right foot forward, touching your kissaki to his left wrist.

Cut forward with your ken.

From this position, your partner can attempt a strike to your left leg. Continue to push forward with your ken, controlling your partner's strike attempt.

Step in to the right with your right foot, maneuvering your partner with your ken to his left wrist as you tenkan to the right.

Force your partner's ken to the mat, pinning your partner's arms as you extend his ken toward the mat.

Practice Points
Maneuvering your partner's sword to the ground is a technique designed to damage it. In the days of the samurai, it was a common practice to wear iron *zori* (sandals) to step on and further damage an enemy's sword. For practice purposes, be careful when pushing your partner's *ken* downward. Even a *bokken* can damage a floor or mat surface.

Ikkyo to *yonkyo ura*—Arm hold techniques (behind)

TAIJUTSU
Example: against *shomen uchi, gyaku hanmi katatedori*, etc.

Shomen uchi—Enter in directly (no initial shinogi movement).

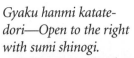

Gyaku hanmi katate-dori—Open to the right with sumi shinogi.

Firmly grab your partner's left hand with your left, and raise his arm upward in an arc counter-clockwise. Place your other hand under his elbow as a brace, rotating his arm forward to take his balance.

Step in to the right, right foot forward, moving your partner in a circular direction as you tenkan.

Spiral your partner downward, taking him to the mat face downward.

3. *Nagare kukuri menuchi sabaki*—Turning *kukuri menuchi sabaki* ○

KENJUTSU
Example: against *tsuki* and *shomen uchi*.

As your partner tsukis …

… open to the right with uchi otoshi shinogi.

As your partner swings up for a second strike, enter right foot forward, cutting forward with your ken on your partner's right wrist.

Pushing in a circular direction, tenkan to the left to avoid a strike to your right leg.

Your partner also tenkans for position. Keep your distance and assume waki gamae with your ken lowered behind you.

As your partner swings up for a third strike, open to the right, and as he strikes downward, strike shomen uchi to the left side of his neck or to his left wrist.

Practice Points

The Japanese word *nagareru* translates as "stream-like," and also to "dissolve." Therefore, when you break apart to avoid a strike to the leg from your partner, your movements in *nagare kukuri* act to dissolve or neutralize what would have been *ura kukuri otoshi sabaki*, had you been able to complete the technique.

Iriminage—Entering throw (behind)

TAIJUTSU

Example: against *shomen uchi, mune tsuki, gyaku hanmi katatedori,* etc.

Shomen uchi—Open to the right with *awase shinogi.*

Mune tsuki—Open to the right with *uchi otoshi shinogi.*

Gyaku hanmi katatedori—Open to the right with *uchi otoshi shinogi.*

Grabbing over your partner's right hand with your right, raise his arm upward clockwise. Slide in right foot forward.

Guide your partner with a firm grasp on his neck with your left hand as you step in with your left foot …

… and complete the tenkan to the left.

As your partner tries to right his balance by standing up, take one more step to throw.

4. Nagare kukuri fukiage sabaki—Turning *kukuri fukiage sabaki* ○

KENJUTSU

Example: against *shomen uchi* (no initial *shinogi* movement).

As your partner swings up to strike …

… match his movement and enter directly.

Slide in, right foot forward, touching your *kissaki* to your partner's right wrist.

Pushing in a circular direction, tenkan to the left to avoid a strike to your right leg.

Your partner also tenkans for position. Keep your distance and assume *waki gamae* with your ken lowered behind you.

As your partner swings up for a third strike, open to the right, and as he strikes downward, cut upward, blade up.

Practice Points

As you *tenkan*, be aware that your partner might be able to use his sword with only his left hand. Keep control of your partner's movements by applying firm pressure on his right wrist with your *ken*. Matching your partner's movements is called *ki musubi*.

Kote gaeishi modified into *iriminage, kokyunage,* to *ago-ate*—
Wrist twist modified into an entering throw or a timing throw with a push to the chin.

TAIJUTSU Example: against *shomen uchi, tsuki, gyaku hanmi katatedori,* etc.

Shomen uchi—Open to the right with awase shinogi.

Tsuki—Open to the right with uchi otoshi shinogi.

Gyaku hanmi katatedori—Move out to the left with kaburi shinogi.

Grab over your partner's right wrist, raising his arm as you slide in, right foot forward. Change hands …

… and tenkan to your left. Guide your partner in a circular direction as you open to the right.

Extend your right hand, and push straight in at his chin …

… as you take one more step and enter to throw.

5. Nagare kukuri makiuchi zuki sabaki—Turning kukuri makiuchi zuki sabaki ○

KENJUTSU

Example: against *shomen uchi* (no initial *shinogi* movement).

Focus on your partner's movement before he swings up to strike.

As your partner swings up to strike shomen uchi, match his movements and enter right foot forward, touching your kissaki to your partner's right wrist.

Cutting forward, pushing in a circular direction, tenkan to the left to avoid a strike to your right leg.

Your partner also tenkans for position. Keep your distance and assume waki gamae with your ken directed behind you.

As your partner tsukis …

… open to the right, and deflect his ken back behind him with a rolling block from underneath, counter-clockwise.

Extend the rolling block (makiuchi zuki) forward until your kissaki is touching your partner's left wrist.

Practice Points

In the word *makiuchi zuki*, *maki* means to wrap or roll up. As your partner *tsukis*, and you begin to utilize *makiuchi zuki* movement, imagine that you are drawing a circle counter-clockwise around your partner's sword from underneath. The circle ends with a glancing strike over his *ken* that forces his *ken* behind him. Your *ken* glances from his *ken* to his left wrist.

Kote gaeshi—Wrist twist

TAIJUTSU Example: against *shomen uchi, mune tsuki,* etc.

Shomen uchi—Enter directly, grabbing over your partner's right wrist (no shinogi movement).

Mune tsuki—Open to the left and grab over your partner's right wrist with uchi otoshi shinogi.

Tenkan to the left, pivoting off your left foot.

Guide your partner in a circular direction as you open to the right.

Raise his arm upward and twist his wrist to the outside, extending his hand toward his body.

Keep a lock on his wrist, turn, and take one more step to throw.

6. *Omote nukidomen sabaki*—Entering *nukidomen sabaki* ○

KENJUTSU

Example: against *tsuki*, *shomen uchi*, and *yokomen uchi*.

Anticipating your
partner's *tsuki* …

… open to the right …

… striking over your
partner's *ken* with
uchi otoshi shinogi.

As your partner swings up
for a second strike, slide right
foot forward in front of your
partner. Cut under his left
armpit with your *kissaki*.

Finish the cut with an
extended pulling motion as
you step in with your left
foot and pivot. Strike
shomen uchi in the same
direction as your partner as
you complete the pivot.

A safe ending position is
slightly behind your partner,
attention focused broadly for
other potential attackers.

Practice Points

When you are cutting under your partner's armpit, your *ken* is held horizontally, even with his armpit. The reason is
that, in theory, your partner would carry
the case for his long sword and a short
sword tucked into his belt on his left side.
If you were to strike at an angle, or too
low, his swords would block the way and
impede the cut.

Shihonage omote—Four-direction throw (front)

TAIJUTSU

Example: against *gyaku hanmi katatedori, ai hanmi katatedori*, etc.

Gyaku hanmi katatedori—
Open to the right with
waki shinogi.

Ai hanmi katatedori—
Open to the right with
uchi otoshi shinogi.

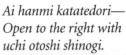

Slide forward in
front of your partner,
right foot forward,
extending his right
arm in front of you
with both hands.

Step in with your
left foot and pivot,
entering with your
hips first.

Finish by extending
your partner's arm
toward the mat as
if you're cutting
downward with
your ken.

7. *Ura mikaeri uchi sabaki*—Turning *mikaeri uchi sabaki* ○

KENJUTSU
Example: against *shomen uchi*.

Anticipating your partner's first strike …

… as your partner swings up to strike shomen uchi, tsuki toward his face as a feint to distract him.

As he strikes downward, open to the right with waki shinogi.

As your partner swings up again for his second strike, match his timing and cut upward from his groin through to his collarbone area in a large arc.

Using the momentum of your upward cut, continue the strike downward as you pivot to the rear, checking for consequent attacks. Swing up again, as you step and pivot again.

Facing the direction of your partner …

… complete your shomen uchi strike.

Practice Points

Mikaeru translates as "to look to the rear or behind you." This technique incorporates an upward cut to your partner's groin and chest area that gives you enough momentum to check behind you before focusing forward once more. This technique is still popular, and is widely used in the Gigen school of *kenjutsu* in Japan.

Shihonage ura—Four-direction throw (behind)*

TAIJUTSU
Example: against *shomen uchi, mune tsuki, kata dori,* etc.

Shomen uchi—Open to the
right with awase shinogi.

Mune tsuki—Open to the right
with uchi otoshi shinogi.

Kata dori—Open to the right
with awase shinogi.

Grabbing your partner's right
wrist with both hands, tenkan to
your left, pivoting on your left foot.
Extend your partner's arm in
front of you.

Tenkan behind your partner,
turning under his extended arm.
Enter with your hips first.

Finish by extending your partner's arm toward the mat as if
you were cutting downward
with your ken.

*There are other taijutsu appli-
cations to this sabaki, including
koshinage or hip throws, that
will be explored in later chapters.

Chapter 5
Kenjutsu to *Taijutsu*
Transitional Relationship Progression Reference

In Chapter 4 we defined both *shinogi* and *sabaki* movements as they relate to *kenjutsu* and *taijutsu*. In this chapter, we will outline a reference guide for understanding the actual relationship between *kenjutsu* and *taijutsu* movements. This guide provides us with a unique tool for exploring these relationships.

Let's try to imagine for a moment an assembly line as an analogy for studying the structure of our Aikido techniques. Imagine raw materials coming off the docks at a manufacturing plant. After the raw materials have been received, they must be sorted for inventory and stored for manufacture. At the proper time, the materials are taken to an assembly line where they are manufactured into a variety of finished products. Your partner's initial attack can be thought of as "raw material." First these movements must be sorted and temporarily stored for further action. This part of the "Aikido assembly line" is our *shinogi* movement. After our partner's movements have been "sorted," they are then ready for the main assembly line. This assembly line can be equated in our Aikido practice with *sabaki* movements. The finished product of this assembly line is one complete Aikido technique. The names of these techniques are made up of both the "raw material" and the name of the assembly line the raw material happened to pass through. For example, if the "raw material *ai hanmi katatedori* (same-hand grab)" were assembled on the *shihonage* assembly line, the finished product or technique would be *ai hanmi katatedori shihonage*.

If either the quality of the raw material itself or the assembly-line process is inferior in any way, the subsequent finished product, or technique, will also be inferior. Your practice and study of Aikido can be thought of as making good finished products out of the raw materials you are given to work with—as smoothly and efficiently as possible. To improve your technique, it is important to be able to clearly define both *shinogi* and *sabaki* movements, and to execute them cleanly and clearly.

In the following pages, a few selected techniques are used to explain the relationship between *kenjutsu* and *taijutsu* more clearly. You will notice there is a middle column between the *kenjutsu* movement on the left and the *taijutsu* movement on the right. This center column illustrates *ken* and open-hand movement together. This is not *tachidori* (sword-taking techniques with an empty hand), but is offered as a visual aid to help you see the transition between each distinct *kenjutsu* and *taijutsu* movement. With a little imagination, however, and a few *atemis* and body blocks, the middle column could be construed as actual techniques! Please compare each photo in all three columns, left to right, to see the similarity of each movement. Remember that all five *shinogi* and seven *sabaki* are made up of △ ○ □ movements. See if you can pick them out.

1. Gyaku hanmi katatedori—Shihonage omote
Opposite-hand grab—Four-direction throw (front)

KENJUTSU

Awase shinogi (to the left) to *nukidomen sabaki.*

TRANSITIONAL MOVEMENT

As your partner swings up to strike *shomen uchi,* begin to move out to the left, matching his breathing as he inhales. As your partner exhales and strikes downward, complete your opening move. As your partner swings up for a second strike, slide across in front of him, right foot forward, and step in with your left foot and pivot.

TAIJUTSU

From a wide distance, your partner grabs your left wrist with his right hand. Adjusting to his speed as he closes the distance, move out to the left. Grab his wrist with your right hand, extending him forward to take his balance. As your partner tries to right himself, slide forward in front of him, right foot forward, extending his arm in front of you. Step in with your left foot and pivot, cutting downward with your hands to throw.

Practice Points

When practicing the technique *shihonage,* you usually end the technique with your partner performing *ushiro ukemi* (back rolls), as illustrated in the photographs (right). Because the purpose of this book is to demonstrate the relationship between *kenjutsu* and *taijutsu,* it is more technically correct to use a break fall as the ending *ukemi.* As you slide across in front, pivot, and throw your partner, if you emulate the actions you would be using with a *ken,* only a break fall can safely protect your partner's shoulder. The correct *kenjutsu* relationship to a standard back roll would be to pivot more slowly, and pause for a moment before gently lowering your elbows in a downward strike.

Kenjutsu   *Transitional*   *Taijutsu*

2. *Ryotedori—Iriminage ura*
Both-hands grab—Entering throw (behind)

KENJUTSU

Kaburi shinogi (to the left) to *nagare kukuri menuchi sabaki.*

TRANSITIONAL MOVEMENT

As your partner strikes *shomen uchi*, move out to the left, arms raised over your head, elbows bent. As he reacts and follows with a subsequent strike, slide in and *tenkan* to the left, arms extended in front of you. Your partner also *tenkans* for position. Once again face to face, as your partner strikes again, open to the right and *atemi* to his face with your right hand.

TAIJUTSU

From a wide distance, as your partner grabs both your wrists with both hands, move out to the left, right foot forward. Raise your arms up and cross your wrists to use as a brace to release your hands from his grab. Arms still raised, slide in right foot forward and *tenkan* to the left, guiding your partner with a firm grasp of his neck or shoulder with your left hand. As he tries to regain his balance by standing, take one more step with your right foot and enter with your whole body to throw.

Practice Points

When practicing the technique *iriminage*, you usually end the technique with your partner performing *ushiro ukemi* (back roll), as illustrated in the photographs to the right. In older styles of jujitsu, this technique is accompanied by blows to the chin, or a severe twisting of your partner's neck. To do *iriminage* in this manner, you need to work with a partner who can provide *ukemi* at a level proficient enough to handle it. You may have seen this technique performed where *nage* (the person executing the technique) applies a straight-arm to his *uke's* (partner's) throat. In response, his *uke* uses his neck for an anchor and swings his legs out from under himself horizontally. This kind of *ukemi* is colorful and decorative but not completely realistic. It is a good move to perform, however, if you are auditioning for a part as a Hollywood stunt-man!

Kenjutsu   *Transitional*   *Taijutsu*

3. Shomen uchi—Kote gaeshi ura
Frontal strike—Wrist twist (behind)

KENJUTSU

No initial *shinogi* movement, beginning directly with *nagare kukuri makiuchi zuki sabaki*.

TRANSITIONAL MOVEMENT

As your partner swings up to strike *shomen uchi,* match his movement, enter right foot forward, and *tenkan* to your left. Your partner also *tenkans* for position. Face to face again, your partner *tsukis*. Open to the right, turn, and enter *(irimi)*.

TAIJUTSU

Enter, right foot forward, and grab over your partner's striking hand with your left hand as you *tenkan* to the left. Guide your partner in a circular direction as you open to the right. Raise his arm upward and twist his wrist to the outside, extending his hand toward his body. Keep a lock on his wrist, turn, and take one more step to throw.

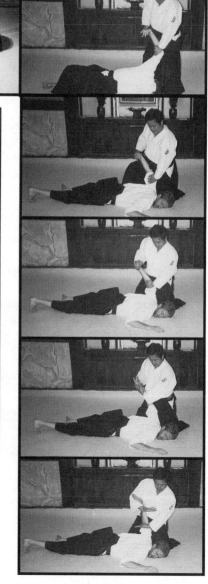

Practice Points
Kote gaeshi **floor pin** (starting from large photo, top right):

Photo 1: Applying pressure to partner's wrist, place your other hand behind his elbow, lifting up slightly as you rotate around his head. You must lift up, or your partner's shoulder will keep him from turning over.

Photo 2: Place your knee snugly between his head and shoulder, pushing down on his elbow.

Photo 3: Place your other knee securely under his armpit, your feet together behind you, toes raised.

Photo 4: Your right hand continues to stimulate partner's wrist.

Photo 5: Move your left arm into position at your partner's elbow, and press forward in a circle counter-clockwise. Your partner signals when enough pressure has been applied by tapping the mat with his free hand.

Kenjutsu   *Transitional*   *Taijutsu*

4. Yokomen uchi—Kote gaeshi ura
Side strike—Wrist twist (behind)

KENJUTSU

Yokomen uchi to *awase shinogi* (to the right), to *kaburi shinogi* (to the left) to *nagare kukuri makiuchi zuki sabaki.* (Photos do not illustrate initial *yokomen uchi* strike, beginning after this initial strike and the *awase shinogi* counter have taken place.)

TRANSITIONAL MOVEMENT

As your partner strikes *yokomen uchi*, open to the right. As he follows with a *tsuki*, move out to the left, hands and elbows raised. Both you and your partner *tenkan*, and face to face again, your partner *tsukis*. Open to the right and enter *(irimi)* from the right side.

TAIJUTSU

Mirror your partner's movement as he strikes *yokomen uchi*, opening to the right. Move out to the left, raising your partner's striking arm with your right hand underneath. Grab over his striking hand with your left hand, slide in, right foot forward, and *tenkan*. Guide your partner in a circular direction as you both turn. Open to the right, and twist his wrist to the outside, extending his hand toward his body. Keep a lock on his wrist, turn, and take one more step to throw.

> ### Practice Points
> In traditional *jujitsu*, wrist twist techniques are accompanied by an *atemi* with a knee as illustrated in the top right photo. The correct way to perform *kote gaeshi* is to roll your partner's hand back toward his body, rather than out to the side. If done correctly, break falls are actually very difficult to do from this technique. If you do twist your partner's wrist away from his body (as shown in the bottom right photo), your partner has the option to do a break fall, or to perform a high round kick to your head or ribs.

Kenjutsu   *Transitional*   *Taijutsu*

5. Gyaku hanmi katatedori—Kokyu nage omote
Opposite-hand grab—Timing throw (front)

KENJUTSU
Sumi shinogi (to the right) followed by entering and touching your kissaki to your partner's left wrist.

TRANSITIONAL MOVEMENT
This technique is a good example of the □ pattern of movement formed by the zigzag footwork.

TAIJUTSU
As your partner grabs your right hand with his left, enter sliding to the right at an angle to take his balance. As you slide, extend your free hand as a brace inside your partner's upper left arm. Step in at an angle with your left foot, entering with your whole body to throw.

> **Practice Points**
> Kokyu nage translates literally as "breath throw." Actually, no one can be thrown with the power of your breath only. Therefore, the definition in the context of Aikido has been changed to "timing throw." This group of techniques (there is a variety of different kokyu nage throws) has been interpreted widely. For example, the kokyu nage illustrated here is called iriminage in some dojos. If you add an atemi to your partner's chin with your free hand, the technique becomes gyaku hanmi katatedori ago ate. If you extend your free hand across your partner's upper chest and neck, it changes the technique to gyaku hanmi katatedori tenchi nage. Adding a leg sweep aimed at your partner's Achilles changes the technique to gyaku hanmi katatedori sumi otoshi.

Kenjutsu

Transitional

Taijutsu

The purpose of this chapter has been to shed some light on the internal structure of all of our Aikido techniques. The similarity of all of the preliminary attacks, *shinogi*, and *sabaki* movements should be clear as you follow the progression from *kenjutsu* through transitional movement to *taijutsu* movement. I hope you can see how important understanding the concepts of *shinogi* and *sabaki* movement can be to your overall understanding of the structure of Aikido.

How to practice *shinogi* movement:

Step 1. Holding your *ken*, assume *migi hanmi* (right stance) and imagine a partner's initial strike. Go over each *shinogi* movement in your mind.

Step 2. Have your partner strike with either *shomen uchi* or *tsuki* and practice all five *shinogi* movements slowly.

Step 3. Hang a piece of wood from the ceiling, suspended by a rope tied around its center. Set the wood in motion, and practice all the *shinogi* movements freely. This type of solitary circuit training is covered in more detail in the third volume of this series.

Step 4. With a partner, practice by adding *sabaki* movement to *shinogi* movements.

How to practice *sabaki* movement:

Step 1. Holding your *ken*, assume *migi hanmi* (right stance) and imagine a partner's initial strike. Go over each *sabaki* movement in your mind.

Step 2. Have your partner strike with either *shomen uchi* or *tsuki*, and practice all *sabaki* movements slowly, without any preliminary *shinogi* movement.

Step 3. With the same piece of hanging wood, set the wood in motion, and practice all the *sabaki* movements freely.

Step 4. With a partner, practice by adding *shinogi* movement to *sabaki* movements.

How to practice open-hand *shinogi* and *sabaki* movement:

Step 1. Sit in *seiza* and try to imagine all five *shinogi* and seven *sabaki* movements in your mind.

Step 2. When you can imagine all of the *shinogi* and *sabaki* movements, hold a pen in your hands as if it were a *ken*, and go through the movements by yourself, slowly.

Step 3. Put the pen down and go through the movements again, this time with your hands empty but correctly holding them in the same position as if you were holding a *ken*.

To practice open-hand *shinogi* and *sabaki* movement, sit in *seiza* and envision each movement done with a partner three-dimensionally. Keep practicing this exercise in *seiza* until you are able to do all of the hand movements with an imaginary *ken* in your hands. Next try this exercise standing, slowly, focusing on the patterns of whole body movement. At Nippon Kan we call this type of practice "Meditation in Motion." It looks a little like Tai Chi when one practices alone, and we have nicknamed it "Ai Chi." Timing your breathing with your movements is important, inhaling as you raise your arms and exhaling as you lower them. Go through the movements rhythmically, as if you were listening to a waltz.

Chapter 6
Ukemi
The Art of Falling

It is very important to learn how to practice *ukemi* safely. Recently there seems to have been a trend in Aikido to practice flamboyant and "acrobatic" *ukemi*. I have seen impressive-looking break falls during demonstrations of techniques like *kote gaeshi, shihonage,* and *iriminage,* for example. This type of stunt *ukemi* is typically used in demonstrations for fun and showmanship. It is important to understand that this type of *ukemi* is just that, stunt work, the likes of which we can find on the Hollywood screen. Unfortunately, many people who do not have a lot of experience practicing Aikido believe that what they see in the movies is real. They think that Aikido techniques can be used as street techniques to throw their enemies into the air at will.

There is, however, a practical purpose for doing break falls when one is practicing with a partner at an advanced level. The purpose is for *uke* to protect his wrists, neck, elbows, and shoulders from injury if a technique is being applied by *nage* correctly, but in an extremely forceful manner. For this type of practice, techniques are performed with an unspoken agreement between parties, each partner consenting to practice at that level of intensity. For this to be successful, it is important that both *uke* and *nage* are at about the same level of expertise and experience. It is not necessary to teach beginners how to do break falls until they have a solid understanding of the basics. Be careful about practicing break falls for fun. Accidents can happen when you are playing around. It is not always necessary to do break falls. Only when they are warranted by the extreme application of a technique should they be used to avoid injury.

This book focuses attention on the body movements used when practicing *kenjutsu* and their inherent relationship to our open-hand techniques. break falls are the correct open-hand correlate to many *kenjutsu* techniques due to the intensity of the delivery of the sword strikes. For general practice, however, break falls are not necessary. Many techniques such as *kokyunage* and *kaitennage,* for example, can be performed, allowing your partner to do a forward roll instead of a break fall by releasing your partner's hand as you throw.

One of the reasons we are able to practice "acrobatic" *ukemi* is because there are no tournaments or competition associated with the practice of Aikido (as it was taught by the founder Morihei Ueshiba). We practice under a set of rules that are designed to avoid injury, even taking turns working on different parts of the techniques together. This type of cooperation is a positive aspect of the practice of Aikido, but it is important to understand that it is this kind of cooperation that enables us to practice "acrobatic" *ukemi*.

Traditional *Jujitsu* does not allow for high "acrobatic" break falls. For example, if *kote gaeshi* is being applied as *Jujitsu* technique, a very low, tight wrist twist is followed by a leg sweep and grappling floor techniques. Choke-holds and joint stimulations are typical endings for *Jujitsu* techniques. What has become modern Judo also utilizes a number of these types of endings in its techniques. Aikido, as it has evolved, has eliminated most grappling floor techniques. This also creates the opportunity to perform "acrobatic" *ukemi*. A more realistic application of *ukemi* would be the use of a front roll to regain position after losing one's balance.

This chapter introduces the most commonly used *ukemi*. To begin practicing *ushiro ukemi* (back rolls), sit in a crossed-leg position, roll backward, then rock forward, returning to a sitting position. For the next step, from the same sitting position, roll backward, and rock forward into a standing position. For beginners, learning to do back rolls from a standing position can be awkward and even painful. This can keep a beginning student from learning smoothly. It is easier to begin to teach *mae ukemi* (front rolls) after new students are comfortable with doing continuous back rolls to a standing position. It is best not to go into too much detail when teaching *ukemi* to beginners, as it only serves to make them think too much about their movements. Thinking too much can make anyone stiff and fearful—which can cause accidents. I have also found that if the instructor demonstrates very high forward rolls or break falls new students have a tendency to try to mimic the instructor's actions—actions they are not quite ready to perform. As this can also result in injuries, it is better to demonstrate small, slow, natural forward rolls as an example for beginners to copy. When teaching someone to swim, you don't start out in the deep water first!

A practical application of ukemi is the use of a front roll to regain position after losing one's balance.

1. *Tachi ushiro ukemi*
Standing back rolls

From a standing position, tuck one foot behind you and roll backward. Then reverse your direction and rock forward again into a standing position. This is the most popularly used *ukemi*.

Tuck one foot behind you, with the outside of your leg and the top of your foot making contact with the mat, as you gently fall backward to the mat.

Roll back onto your hip.

Tuck your head forward as if you were trying to see into your navel.

Using your legs for momentum, roll back, keeping your head tucked forward.

Rock forward again to a standing position, with your foot tucked behind you in the same position.

Stand up, back straight, tuck the other foot, and repeat to the other side.

2. *Ushiro mawari dachi ukemi*
Back rolls to a standing position

Roll backward, letting your momentum carry you completely over, returning to a standing position.

Tuck one foot behind you, with the outside of your leg and the top of your foot making contact with the mat as you gently fall backward to the mat.

Curve your back into a rounded shape, and tuck your head forward.

As your feet go over your head, turn your head to the side. (Which side depends on which foot you have tucked behind you. Right foot tucked, turn your head to the left, and vice versa.) This is to avoid going straight over the back of your neck and head.

If you tucked your left foot and turned your head to the right, you will roll over your right shoulder naturally. Continue to roll over until your knee touches the mat.

Push yourself up …

… until you have returned to a standing position.

3. *Mae ukemi*
Front rolls

Front rolls beginning and ending in a standing position.

From a standing position, extend your left hand and left foot forward.

Touching the outside edge of your hand to the mat first, extend your arm into a rounded arc. It is important to have your arm extended correctly, so do this under supervision only.

Roll forward, keeping your arm extended and your head tucked.

Continue to roll over your left shoulder and right hip naturally.

As you complete the roll, tuck your leg underneath you with the top of your foot in contact with the mat.

Push yourself forward and up to a standing position.

The *ukemi* practiced in *taijutsu* was originally used when falling with a sword in one's hands. This can also be practiced by repeating the previous exercises holding a *ken*.

Mae ukemi

Ushiro ukemi

Chapter 7
Ken Tai Icchi No Ugoki
Kenjutsu and *Taijutsu* Movement in Unison

The *kenjutsu* and *taijutsu* relationships introduced in this chapter form the base of Nippon Kan's original teaching method. I first introduced this teaching method in the United States in 1984 through a video series that was distributed throughout the United States and Europe.

To be pragmatic, only a few techniques have been used in this chapter to illustrate *kenjutsu* to *taijutsu* movement relationships. For example, the technique *katatedori shihonage* (one-hand grab—four-direction throw) can be executed at least twelve different ways, depending on if you are working to the front or the back, and which variation of hand movement you use. To explain the *kenjutsu* relationship to each of these variations in one volume would be impractical. Instead, I have selected a variety of the most popular Aikido open-hand techniques to use as examples.

Our open-hand Aikido movement must also take into consideration the possibility of multiple attackers. To illustrate this possibility, a second attacker is included in some of the examples *(tateki no kurai)*. The response to any given attack depends greatly on the distance from which a partner is attacking. *Nage* moves in response to the movements of his partners, and must adjust his or her movements to match the speed and position of each attack individually. The following descriptions are only examples, since each practice is individually distinct, with its own set of variables.

Because of the space limitations set by the size of the picture frame, *nage* and his partners are portrayed close together *(gobu no mawai)* for each technique. Please note by the written descriptions that some of the techniques are meant for a wide distance approach.

To avoid confusion, most of the techniques illustrated are executed on the right side only. Keep in mind, however, that while the *ken* is always held with the right hand forward and the left hand to the rear, each technique with minor adjustments can be performed to the left side as well.

Analyzing our open-hand relationships by studying how *nage* responds to each attack with *shinogi* or *sabaki* movement is a relatively new field of study. It has been a study I have enjoyed as I worked to develop Nippon Kan's teaching method. I look forward to the further development of this new field of study of *kenjutsu* to *taijutsu* relationships.

Katame Waza
Grappling Techniques

Katame waza (grappling techniques) are an integral part of Aikido that originates from the traditional art of Jujitsu. One characteristic that distinguishes this group of techniques is that *uke* is pinned face down to the mat at the completion of each technique. Originally this group of techniques was used to render an attacker unable to counter-attack from the ground with a hidden weapon, or to strike back from a face-up position. There are five *katame waza* most commonly practiced in Aikido, the first basic *katame waza* being *dai ikkyo ude osae* (first arm hold). In most traditional *dojos* new students begin their study of Aikido with this technique. The movements encompassed in this technique are essential to the foundation of all of *kihon* (basic) Aikido movement.

The likeness of movement between *taijutsu* and *kenjutsu* is illustrated in the most basic of *katame waza*: *shomen uchi—ude osae* (frontal strike—arm hold). Arm hold techniques, beginning with a *yokomen uchi* strike, also follow the same pattern of movement whether they are done open-handed or with a *ken*.

In *kenjutsu*, this group of techniques utilizes either *omote kukuri otoshi sabaki* (front), or *ushiro kukuri otoshi sabaki* (behind). These techniques actually end with a body block to take your partner's balance, followed by a *tsuki* to finish. In this book, however, the final *tsuki* to finish has been omitted, ending each technique by pinning your partner's *ken* to the mat. As you enter to perform this technique, it is possible to end up locked *tsuba* to *tsuba* with your partner's *ken*. This form of combat is called *tsuba zeriai*. Traditionally, kicks to the knee or foot-sweeps were used to counter this type of stalemate.

Some Aikidoists believe that Aikido does not require physical conditioning. I do not agree, however, and think that general body conditioning with sit-ups, light weights, and *suburi*, etc., is of great benefit. Basic training for *katame waza* can be done by practicing *suburi* with a *suburito* (an oversized heavy *bokken* used to develop physical muscular power). Another useful exercise is to do push-ups with the outside edge of your hand (blade of your hand) extended vertically in contact with the mat.

In kenjutsu, katame waza (grappling techniques) use omote kukuri otoshi sabaki (front) or ushiro kukuri otoshi sabaki (behind).

Ude Osae
Arm Hold Techniques

1. *Shomen uchi—Ikkyo omote*
Frontal strike—First arm hold (front)

STRUCTURE □
No initial *shinogi* movement, beginning directly with *omote kukuri otoshi sabaki*.

KENJUTSU

As your partner swings up to strike *shomen uchi*, match his timing and slide in, right foot forward, cutting forward with your *kissaki* to your partner's right wrist, breaking his balance. Continue to slide right foot forward in front of your partner, using your *ken* to push him forward, forcing his *ken* to the mat with *omote kukuri otoshi sabaki*. After your partner has been immobilized, finish with a left knee or kick to the ribs, or take one more step with your left foot for a body block.

TAIJUTSU

Enter in as your partner swings up to strike *shomen uchi* with his right hand. Slide in front of your partner, right foot forward. Arms extended, push forward using your left hand under your partner's elbow as a brace. Rotate his arm in a circular motion downward toward the mat. Take one more step in with your left foot for a body block, forcing your partner face down to the mat. Depending on which hand position you use, this technique can be either *ikkyo* or *nikyo* (second arm hold).

Practice Points

When doing this technique it is very important to slide in front of your partner with your "outside" leg, or the leg that is farthest away from him. Only after you have gained control over your partner by rotating his arm and upper body forward into a horizontal position is it safe to step in with your "inside" leg, or the leg closest to him. If you step in first with your "inside" leg, without first gaining control over your partner, it allows him the opportunity to grab your leg. It is also difficult to complete the technique with a body block or a knee to the ribs if your weight is already on your "inside" foot. When practicing this technique open-handed, do not grab your partner's elbow tightly like an eagle would grab with its claws. Instead use the extended outside edge and palm of your hand to apply forward pressure under the elbow. This hand position is called *han nigiri* and is commonly seen in traditional Jujitsu techniques.

Kenjutsu

Taijutsu

2. *Shomen uchi—Ikkyo ura*
Frontal strike—First arm hold (behind)

STRUCTURE ○

No initial *shinogi* movement, beginning directly with *ushiro kukuri otoshi sabaki.*

KENJUTSU

As your partner swings up to strike *shomen uchi*, match his timing and enter, right foot forward. Cut forward with your *kissaki* to your partner's left wrist, breaking his balance. *Tenkan* to the right, applying continual pressure to your partner's wrist with a forward cut with your *ken*. Move your partner in a circular direction until his *ken* is forced to the mat with *ushiro kukuri otoshi sabaki.* After your partner has been immobilized, finish with a right knee or kick to the ribs, or take one more step with your right foot for a body block.

TAIJUTSU

As your partner swings up to strike *shomen uchi* with his left hand, slide in, arms extended, with your left foot forward. Extend your partner's arm forward toward his head, using your right hand as a brace under his elbow. Keep your arms extended as you *tenkan* to the right, taking your partner toward the mat in a circular motion. Keep all of your body weight over your partner's arm as you complete the technique with your partner face down on the mat.

Practice Points

Use your whole body as you make initial contact with your partner by sliding inward as he or she is swinging up to strike. As you do this, enter in with your arms extended but not locked in a straight position. If your elbows are locked, your partner's momentum can cause him to deflect off your hands. Having your arms extended but not locked offers a cushion for the force of your partner's initial movement and absorbs some of the shock of the strike. A hanging heavy bag is useful for practicing this entering move. Extend forward toward the bag with your arms extended, but slightly rounded.

Kenjutsu   *Taijutsu*

3. *Shomen uchi—Ikkyo omote*
Frontal strike—First arm hold (front, opening to the inside)

STRUCTURE △ ○
Awase shinogi to *omote kukuri otoshi sabaki.*

KENJUTSU

As your partner swings up to strike *shomen uchi,* match his movement. As he strikes downward, open to the right with *awase shinogi.* As your partner swings up for a second strike, slide in with a forward cut to his right wrist with your *kissaki.* Follow with *omote kukuri otoshi sabaki,* until his *ken* is forced to the mat. This kind of matched movement was called *ki musubi* by the founder, Morihei Ueshiba.

TAIJUTSU

As your partner swings up to strike *shomen uchi* with his right hand, open to the right. As he strikes downward, cover his hand with your right hand, extending pressure downward to take his balance. (If you grab and twist his hand at this point, the technique becomes *nikyo.*) As he rocks backward to regain his balance, slide forward in front of him, right foot forward. Raising his arm upward in an arc clockwise, use your left hand as a brace under his elbow to rotate his arm forward. Take one more step inward with your left foot, taking him to the mat. Use the power of your hips in executing this technique.

Practice Points

When making your initial opening move to the right, it is not necessary to take large unnatural steps. Normal steps will allow you enough room to get off the line of attack. Just moving your upper body, however, without taking any steps, is not enough. Make sure you are still facing your partner as you move off the line of attack. While you are practicing open-handed, make sure as *uke* that your arm is extended as you strike. If your arm is slack, as *nage* enters with his hand at your elbow, his thumb may end up in your eye.

Kenjutsu

Taijutsu

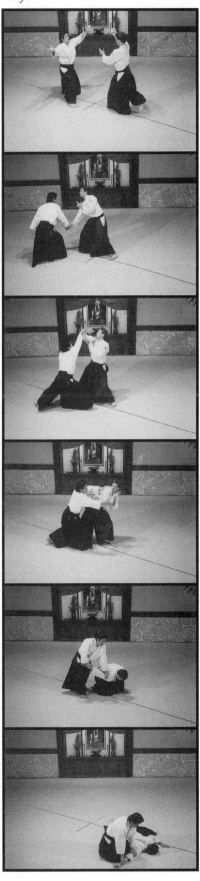

4. *Ai hanmi katatedori—Ikkyo omote*
Same-hand grab—First arm hold (front)

STRUCTURE △ ○

Waki shinogi to *omote kukuri otoshi sabaki.*

KENJUTSU

As your partner swings up to strike *shomen uchi, tsuki* toward his face as a feint to distract him. As he strikes downward, open to the right with *waki shinogi.* As your partner swings up for a second strike, slide in, right foot forward, and cut to his right wrist with your *kissaki.* Push forward with your *ken* with *omote kukuri otoshi sabaki,* until his *ken* is forced to the mat. Finish with a left knee or kick to the ribs, or take one more step with your left foot for a body block.

TAIJUTSU

From a wide distance, your partner grabs for your right wrist with his right hand. Offer your hand to him palm down as you open to the right. As he grabs your wrist, rock backward to take his balance. As he tries to regain his balance, enter sliding forward in front of him, right foot forward. Using your left hand under his elbow as a brace, rotate his arm forward until all of your body weight is over his upper arm. This will leave him unable to regain a standing position. Once he has been immobilized, take one more step with your left foot inward toward your partner, forcing him face down to the mat. If your partner approaches from a closer distance, there is no time for an opening *shinogi* movement. It is better to enter directly with *omote kukuri otoshi sabaki.*

Practice Points

For both *waki shinogi* and *kaburi shinogi,* you use your *ken* to *tsuki* toward your partner's face as he or she swings up to strike. This *tsuki* is not meant to make actual contact with your partner's face. Instead it is used as a feint to distract him from the fact that you are moving off the line of attack. When practicing *taijutsu,* an *atemi* can also be used as a feint to distract. If your intention is to use an *atemi* to strike your partner's face as an opening move, possibly one of the other striking martial arts might be more suited to you.

Kenjutsu

Taijutsu

5. Ushiro ryotekubidori—Ikkyo omote
Behind-both-wrists grab—First arm hold (front)

STRUCTURE ○

No initial *shinogi* movement, beginning directly with *nukidomen sabaki* to *omote kukuri otoshi sabaki*.

KENJUTSU

As your partner swings up to strike *shomen uchi, tsuki* toward his face as a feint to distract him. As he strikes downward, slide in front of your partner, right foot forward, cutting under his left armpit with *nukidomen sabaki*. Use only the *kissaki*, or the first few inches of the tip of your *ken*, to cut under his arm. As you *tenkan*, your partner also *tenkans* for position. Face to face again, your partner swings up for a second strike. Slide in with a forward cut to his left wrist and follow with *omote kukuri otoshi sabaki*, forcing his *ken* to the mat.

TATEKI NO KURAI

Both partners swing up to strike *shomen uchi* from the front and from behind. As your first partner swings up to strike, slide across in front of him, right foot forward, cutting under his left armpit with *nukidomen sabaki*. *Tenkan* to face your second partner, *ken* directed toward him. Your first partner also *tenkans* for position, and is now also face to face with you. As your first partner swings up for a second strike, slide in with a forward cut to his left wrist and follow with *omote kukuri otoshi sabaki* until his *ken* is forced to the mat. In this position, your first partner acts as a barrier between you and your second partner.

TAIJUTSU

As your partner approaches to grab both of your hands from behind, offer your left hand, palm up. Extend your arm forward and upward in front of you, as you *tenkan* to the right under his arm *(uchi tenkan)*. As your partner comes around again in front of you, use your right hand under his elbow to rotate his arm forward, taking him to the mat.

Kenjutsu	Tateki no kurai	Taijutsu

Kenjutsu, continued

Tateki no kurai, continued

Taijutsu, continued

6. *Gyaku hanmi katatedori—Nikyo ura*
Opposite-hand grab—Second arm hold (behind)

STRUCTURE △ ○
Kaburi shinogi to *ushiro kukuri otoshi sabaki.*

KENJUTSU

As your partner swings up to strike *shomen uchi, tsuki* toward his face as a feint to distract him. As he strikes downward, move out to the right and cover with *kaburi shinogi.* As your partner swings up for a second strike, slide in left foot forward, touching your *kissaki* to your partner's left wrist. *Tenkan* to the right, applying continual pressure to your partner's wrist with a forward cut with your *ken.* Move your partner in a circular direction until his *ken* is forced to the mat with *ushiro kukuri otoshi sabaki.* Finish with a right knee or kick to the ribs, or take one more step in with your right foot for a body block.

TATEKI NO KURAI

Both partners strike *shomen uchi* from the front and from behind. Distract your first partner as he swings up to strike with a *tsuki* toward his face, and open to the right with *kaburi shinogi* as both partners strike downward. Enter in, left foot forward, as your first partner swings up for a second strike, cutting forward with your *kissaki* to his left wrist. As you *tenkan,* immobilizing your first partner with *ushiro kukuri otoshi sabaki,* he becomes a defensive barrier between you and your second partner.

TAIJUTSU

From a wide distance your partner approaches to grab your right hand with his left hand. Extend your right hand toward him as you move out to the right. Just as he grabs your hand, peel his hand from yours by grabbing over his hand with your left. Swinging his arm upward counter-clockwise, slide in left foot forward and *tenkan* to the right. As you turn, use your right hand under his elbow to rotate him forward in a circular direction toward the mat. While turning your partner as you *tenkan,* if he tries to right his balance and stand up, you can use his momentum and the grip you have on his left hand to apply a *nikyo* stimulation to regain control. The *nikyo* pin shown in the last photo illustrates the correct *kenjutsu* to *taijutsu* relationship.

Practice Points

In *kenjutsu,* your body posture is very important, even while anticipating the initial strike of your partner. Standing in right *hanmi,* your weight should be distributed with about 70 percent of it on your back foot. This leaves your front foot balanced on the mat, lightly enough so you could easily draw a picture with your toes. From this position you can readily push off from your back foot and move with agility—like a cat crouched, waiting to pounce on a mouse.

Kenjutsu

Tateki no kurai

Taijutsu

Nage Waza
Throwing Techniques

The most commonly practiced throwing techniques include *shihonage* (four-direction throw), *iriminage* (entering body throw), *tenchinage* (sky and ground throw), *kaitennage* (rolling throw), *jujinage* (crossed-arm throw), *koshinage* (hip throw), *tembinnage* (leveraged arm throw), and *kokyunage* (timing throws).

All of these throwing techniques can be divided into two categories. The first category includes techniques that use a joint stimulation to the elbow or shoulder at the beginning of the throw. *Shihonage, jujinage,* and *tembinnage* are examples of techniques that fall into this category. *Shihonage* or *jujinage* can be modified into *koshinage* or *kokyunage* as variations. This type of modification is called *henka waza* (modified techniques).

The second category includes techniques that manipulate the neck and head area. As examples, *tenchinage* utilizes *ago ate* (upward push to the chin) as you draw your partner's body toward you as you enter, then reverse directions to throw. When executing *iriminage*, your partner's head is rotated with your arm as you reverse directions to throw. The manner in which these techniques are practiced today has evolved to protect *uke* from injury during daily practice.

Shihonage is not only specific to Aikido, as a variety of related techniques can be found in traditional Jujitsu under different names. *Kokyunage,* on the other hand, has been widely developed in recent Aikido history as its practice has become popular for use in "high-flying" demonstrations. I have seen *kokyunage* throws demonstrated by instructors who had their *ukes* grab onto a towel held in their hand, or onto one of their fingers as they threw them high into the air. I have seen demonstrations where the instructor did not even touch his *ukes* and he sent them flying. This kind of performance is an audience pleaser but does not convey the truth of what is being demonstrated. Representing Aikido on such premises is offering illusion.

When practicing these throwing techniques, always be aware of your partner's level of ability and experience. Do not throw your partner faster or harder than he or she is able to respond to. A one-second accident can easily cause an extended hiatus from practice.

Shihonage
Four-direction throw

1. Gyaku hanmi katatedori—Shihonage omote
Opposite-hand grab—Four-direction throw (front)

STRUCTURE △ ○

Waki shinogi to *nukidomen sabaki.*

KENJUTSU

From a wide distance, as your partner swings up to strike *shomen uchi, tsuki* toward his face as a feint to distract him. As he strikes downward, open to the right with *waki shinogi.* As your partner swings up again for a second strike, slide across in front of your partner, right foot forward, cutting under his left armpit as you step and pivot with *nukidomen sabaki.* As your partner completes his second unavailing strike, from your adjusted position complete your strike downward in the same direction. In *kenjutsu, nukidomen sabaki* is utilized in the *ken no shiho giri* (four-direction cut) and the *happo giri* (eight-direction cut). This technique is a particularly good example of the likeness of motion between *kenjutsu* and *taijutsu.*

TAIJUTSU

Reach toward your partner as he approaches, opening to the right as he grabs your left hand with his right. Breaking his balance with your opening move, slide forward in front of your partner, right foot forward, holding his arm extended in front of you as you step and pivot. As you pivot, use your hips and cut downward with your hands to throw.

Kenjutsu   *Taijutsu*

Kenjutsu, continued   *Taijutsu, continued*

2. *Katatedori ryotemochi—Shihonage omote*
   Two-hands-on-one grab—Four-direction throw (front)

STRUCTURE △ ○

Awase shinogi to *nukidomen sabaki.*

KENJUTSU

As your partner swings up to strike *shomen uchi,* enter with your *ken* poised in front of you until you are locked together with your partner's *ken* at the area where the *tsuba* or sword guard would be found. Push over the top of your partner's *ken,* forcing his *kissaki* away from you, back behind him to his right. At the same time, move out to the right with *awase shinogi.* As he swings up again, slide across in front of your partner, right foot forward, cutting under his left armpit as you step, pivot, and strike downward to complete *nukidomen sabaki.*

TAIJUTSU

You initiate contact by first striking *shomen uchi* with your right hand. Your partner blocks this strike with his right hand and guides your hand downward where he can grab your wrist with both hands. Extending your right hand and grabbing his right wrist with your left hand, slide right foot forward in front of your partner. Holding his arm extended in front of you, step and pivot. As you pivot, use your hips and cut downward with your hands to throw.

Practice Points

The Japanese word *nuki* translates as "to draw" (as in drawing a sword). *Do* is the Japanese word for trunk or torso. This is not a literal translation, however. *Nukido* does not mean cutting through someone's torso. *Nukidomen* is a cut made with your *kissaki* to the vulnerable area of your partner's armpit just before you step and pivot. The reason more of the blade is not used to try to inflict a deep cut to your partner's belly or side is because traditionally the samurai carried both the case for their long sword and their *wakizashi* (short sword) on the left side. These cases, secured in their belts on their left sides, served as an obstruction to any such deep cut to the torso. You may question why the samurai did not simply throw away the sword case after a battle had begun. They did not do this because it was considered bad luck. It implied that the samurai would not have further need for his sword case, which meant that he would die in battle.

Kenjutsu   *Taijutsu*

Kenjutsu, continued   *Taijutsu, continued*

3. *Shomen uchi—Shihonage omote*
Frontal strike—Four-direction throw (front)

STRUCTURE △ ○
Waki shinogi to *nukidomen sabaki*.

KENJUTSU

As your partner swings up to strike *shomen uchi*, *tsuki* toward his face as a feint to distract him. As he strikes downward, open to the right with *waki shinogi*. As he swings up again for a second strike, slide across in front of him, right foot forward, cutting under his left armpit as you step, pivot, and strike downward to complete *nukidomen sabaki*. The *waki shinogi* movement illustrated is the response to a strike from a close distance. If there is more distance to work with, the response would be to open, bringing your *ken* to your left side with the *kissaki* pointed behind you with *waki shinogi*.

TATEKI NO KURAI

As both partners swing up to strike *shomen uchi* from the front and from behind, *tsuki* toward your first partner's face. Open to the right with *waki shinogi* as both partners strike downward, avoiding both strikes. As both partners swing up for a second strike, slide across in front of your first partner, right foot forward, cutting under his left armpit. Step, pivot, and strike downward to complete *nukidomen sabaki*, training your attention on your second partner.

TAIJUTSU

As your partner strikes *shomen uchi* with his right hand, capture his hand with your left hand on top of his and your right hand underneath. Open to the right and slide forward in front of your partner, holding his arm extended in front of you. Slide right foot forward, step, and pivot. As you pivot use your hips and cut downward with your hands to throw.

Practice Points
When making the cut to your partner's armpit, do not use more than the last few inches of your *kissaki*. If you use the lower portions of the cutting edge of the blade, as you attempt to pivot your *ken* will become lodged, and you will not be able to turn. To avoid this, keep enough distance between you to use only the *kissaki*. The armpit is targeted because it is one of the areas not covered with the protective armor worn by the samurai. Also, a cut to this area could cause enough damage for your opponent to have to surrender, without causing a mortal wound.

Kenjutsu

Tateteki no kurai

Taijutsu

Kenjutsu, continued

Tateki no kurai, continued

Taijutsu, continued

4. *Shomen uchi—Shihonage ura*
Frontal strike—Four-direction throw (behind)

STRUCTURE △ ○

Awase shinogi to *mikaeri uchi sabaki* to *nukidomen sabaki.*

KENJUTSU

As your partner swings up to strike *shomen uchi, tsuki* toward his face as a feint to distract him. As he strikes downward, open to the right with *awase shinogi.* As your partner swings up again for a second strike, step to the left with your left foot forward and cut under his right armpit as you *tenkan* with *mikaeri uchi sabaki.* Pivot and strike downward, this time facing opposite directions, to complete *nukidomen sabaki.*

TAIJUTSU

As your partner strikes *shomen uchi* with his right hand, capture his hand with your left hand on top of his and your right hand underneath. Raise his arm upward as you step to the left of your partner's front foot with your left foot to *tenkan.* Pivot and cut downward with your hands to throw.

> **Practice Points**
> There is a higher percentage of injuries associated with *shihonage ura.* Be especially careful as you raise your partner's arm and *tenkan.* If you are concentrating only on the throw at this point and move too quickly, you can over-extend your partner's arm, causing damage to his or her shoulder.

Kenjutsu   *Taijutsu*

Kenjutsu, continued

Taijutsu, continued

5. *Yokomen uchi—Shihonage omote*
Side strike—Four-direction throw (front)

STRUCTURE △ △ ○

Awase shinogi to *uchi otoshi shinogi* to *nukidomen sabaki.*

KENJUTSU

As your partner strikes *yokomen uchi*, match his movements with *awase shinogi* as you open to the right. As he follows directly with a *tsuki*, block with *uchi otoshi shinogi*, pushing his *ken* back behind him to the right as you open again slightly to the right. As he swings up again for a third strike, slide across in front of him, right foot forward, cutting under his left armpit as you step and pivot, striking downward to complete *nukidomen sabaki.*

TATEKI NO KURAI

Your first partner strikes *yokomen uchi* from the front, as your second partner strikes *shomen uchi* from behind. Match your first partner's movements with *awase shinogi* as you open to the right, avoiding your second partner's strike. Your first partner follows with a *tsuki*, while your second partner strikes *shomen uchi*. Open again to the right with *uchi otoshi shinogi* in response to your first partner's *tsuki*, while avoiding the second strike of your second partner. As both partners swing up again for a third strike, slide across in front of your first partner, right foot forward, cutting under his left armpit as you step and pivot. As you pivot, strike downward to complete *nukidomen sabaki*, training your attention on your second partner.

TAIJUTSU

As your partner strikes *yokomen uchi* with his right hand, match his movements, opening to the right as you guide his hand downward in front of you with your left hand. With both hands holding your partner's wrist, extend your partner's arm forward to take his balance, and slide forward in front of him, Keeping his arm extended in front of you, slide right foot forward, step, and pivot. As you pivot, use your hips and cut downward with your hands to throw.

Practice Points

To do this technique correctly, it is important once you have grabbed your partner's wrist, to slide first on your "outside" foot before you step and pivot (see *taijutsu* photos 2 and 3, page 91). If you step too soon with your "inside" foot, your partner has a chance to sweep that leg out from under you. When practicing *kenjutsu*, if you do not slide with your "outside" foot first before you step and pivot, you will pivot right in front of your partner, leaving yourself vulnerable to a cut from behind.

Kenjutsu

Tateki no kurai

Taijutsu

Kenjutsu, continued

Tateki no kurai, continued

Taijutsu, continued

6. *Katadori shomen uchi—Shihonage omote*
One-hand shoulder grab with a frontal strike—Four-direction throw (front)

STRUCTURE △ ○

Waki shinogi to *nukidomen sabaki*.

KENJUTSU

As your partner swings up to strike *shomen uchi*, *tsuki* toward his face as a feint to distract him. As he strikes downward, open to the right with *waki shinogi*. As your partner swings up again for a second strike, slide across in front of him, right foot forward, cutting under his left armpit as you step and pivot, striking downward to complete *nukidomen sabaki*.

TAIJUTSU

Extend your right hand toward your partner's face as he grabs your right shoulder with his left hand and raises his right hand to strike *shomen uchi*. As he strikes, open to the right, guiding his striking hand downward in front of your center with your right hand underneath and your left hand on top. Extend your partner's arm to take his balance, and slide forward in front of him holding his arm extended in front of you. Slide right foot forward, step, and pivot. As you pivot use your hips and cut downward with your hands to throw.

> **Practice Points**
> When practicing the technique *shihonage*, hand and body movement varies slightly depending on your *ma-ai* (the distance between you and your partner) at the beginning of the technique. For *gyaku hanmi katatedori* alone, there are more than seven slight variations depending on distance. Most of the techniques illustrated in this book are responses to attacks from a distance of one full body length, arms outstretched (*gobo no ma-ai*), to two full body lengths, arms outstretched (*toma no ma-ai*).

Kenjutsu   *Taijutsu*

Kenjutsu, continued   *Taijutsu, continued*

7. Ushiro ryotekubidori—Shihonage ura
Behind-both-wrists grab—Four-direction throw (behind)

STRUCTURE △ ○ ○

Waki shinogi to *nukidomen sabaki* to *nukidomen sabaki.*

KENJUTSU

From a wide distance, as your partner *tsukis*, open to the left with *waki shinogi*. As your partner swings up for a second strike, slide to the left, left foot forward, and *tenkan*, cutting under his right armpit. Your partner also *tenkans* for position. Face to face again, your partner swings up for a second strike. This time slide in front of your partner, right foot forward, cutting under his left armpit as you step and pivot, striking downward to complete *nukidomen sabaki*.

TATEKI NO KURAI

Your first partner *tsukis* from the front as your second partner strikes *shomen uchi* from behind. Open to the left with *waki shinogi,* avoiding the strikes of both partners. As both partners swing up again for a second strike, slide to the left of your first partner and *tenkan,* cutting under his right armpit. He also *tenkans* for position. Face to face again, both partners swing up for a third strike. Slide across in front of your first partner, left foot forward, step and pivot with *nukidomen sabaki.* Your first partner acts as a defensive barrier between you and your second partner.

TAIJUTSU

From a wide distance your partner approaches to grab your right hand with both hands. Extend your hand to him palm down, as you open to the left. Step under your partner's raised arm to the left and *tenkan*. As your partner follows your lead to a face-to-face position, offer your left hand for him to grab. With both hands, extend his arm in front of you and slide across in front of him, left foot forward, step, and pivot. Using your hips, cut downward with your hands to throw.

Kenjutsu	*Tateki no kurai*	*Taijutsu*

Kenjutsu, continued

Tateki no kurai, continued

Taijutsu, continued

Iriminage
Entering throw

1. Shomen uchi—Iriminage ura #1
Frontal strike—Entering throw (behind)

STRUCTURE ○ △

No initial *shinogi* movement, beginning directly with *nagare kukuri menuchi sabaki*.

KENJUTSU

As your partner swings up to strike *shomen uchi*, enter sliding in right foot forward and touch your *kissaki* to your partner's right wrist. Pushing in a circular direction, *tenkan* to the left to avoid a strike to your right leg, as your partner also *tenkans* for position. Face to face again, your partner swings up for his second strike. Open to the right and strike *shomen uchi* to complete *nagare kukuri menuchi sabaki*.

TATEKI NO KURAI

Both partners strike *shomen uchi* from the front and from behind. As your first partner swings up to strike, slide in right foot forward, touching your *kissaki* to his right wrist. As you slide forward to counter your first partner's strike, you move yourself out of the striking range of your second partner. Both you and your first partner *tenkan* until you are positioned again face to face. As both partners swing up for a second strike, open to the right and strike *shomen uchi* to complete *nagare kukuri menuchi sabaki*.

TAIJUTSU

As your partner raises his right hand to strike *shomen uchi*, slide in right foot forward until you have made contact with his right wrist with your right hand. *Tenkan* to the left, guiding your partner with a firm grasp of his neck or shoulder with your left hand. As your partner tries to regain the balance he lost through the momentum of the turn, take one more step forward with your right foot and enter with your whole body to throw.

Practice Points

Nagare kukuri menuchi sabaki is actually the continuation of *ushiro kukuri otoshi sabaki*. During initial contact there is a lot of force pitted between both partners, and *ushiro kukuri otoshi sabaki* is one technique utilized to harness that force. If your partner breaks away from you with a *tenkan* as you attempt this technique, the technique becomes *nagare kukuri menuchi sabaki*. The initial entering movement is called *ikkyo joge undo* and is described in more detail in *Children and the Martial Arts: An Aikido Point of View* (North Atlantic Books, 1993). Keep in mind that the initial contact is not a block but a starting point for redirecting your partner's energy and momentum. In this case, your partner's momentum is redirected into a *tenkan* to the left. In more traditional styles of Jujitsu there are many variations for the beginning of the throw (pictured in the *taijutsu* column, photo 5). A more traditional approach might be to hold your partner's head between your hands and twist, push to his chin with the blade of your hand, or add a foot sweep.

Kenjutsu

Tateki no kurai

Taijutsu

2. Shomen uchi—Iriminage ura #2
Frontal strike—Entering throw (behind)

STRUCTURE △ ○ △

Awase shinogi to *nagare kukuri menuchi sabaki.*

KENJUTSU

Match your partner's movement as he swings up to strike *shomen uchi.* As he strikes downward, open to the right with *awase shinogi.* As he swings up again for a second strike, enter, sliding in right foot forward, and touch your *kissaki* to your partner's right wrist. Pushing in a circular direction, *tenkan* to the left to avoid a strike to your right leg, as your partner also *tenkans* for position. Face to face again, your partner swings up for his third strike. Open to the right and strike *shomen uchi* to complete *nagare kukuri menuchi sabaki.*

TAIJUTSU

As your partner swings up to strike with his right hand, open to the right. As he strikes downward, cover his right hand with yours, extending pressure downward to take him forward off balance. As he rocks backward to regain his balance, raise his arm up in an arc clockwise, and *tenkan* to the left, guiding your partner with a firm grasp of his neck or shoulder with your left hand. As your partner tries to regain his balance by standing, take one more step forward with your right foot and enter with your whole body to throw.

Kenjutsu

Taijutsu

Kenjutsu, continued   *Taijutsu, continued*

3. *Gyaku hanmi katatedori—Iriminage ura*
Opposite-hand grab—Entering throw (behind)

STRUCTURE △ ○ △

Kaburi shinogi to *nagare kukuri menuchi sabaki.*

KENJUTSU

As your partner swings up to strike *shomen uchi*, *tsuki* toward his face as a feint to distract him. As he strikes downward, move out to the left and cover with *kaburi shinogi*. As he swings up again for a second strike, enter, sliding in right foot forward, and touch your *kissaki* to your partner's right wrist. Pushing in a circular direction, *tenkan* to the left, as your partner also *tenkans* to regain position. Face to face again, your partner swings up for his third strike. Open to the right and strike *shomen uchi* to complete *nagare kukuri menuchi sabaki.*

TATEKI NO KURAI

Both partners strike *shomen uchi* from the front and from behind. Distract your first partner as he swings up to strike with a *tsuki* toward his face, and move out to the left with *kaburi shinogi* as both partners strike downward. Enter in as both partners swing up for a second strike, touching your first partner's right wrist with your *kissaki*. *Tenkan* to the left, repositioning yourself face to face with both partners. As both partners swing up for a third strike, open to the right and strike *shomen uchi* toward your second partner's neck or wrist.

TAIJUTSU

As your partner approaches from a wide distance, extend your left hand toward him. As he grabs, move out to the left and cover with your right foot in front. Raise your arms up and cross your wrists to use as a brace to release your hand from your partner's grasp. Arms still raised, guide your partner's right arm with your right hand as you slide, and *tenkan* to the left. As you turn, grasp his shoulder or neck with your left hand. As your partner tries to regain his balance by standing, take one more step forward with your right foot and enter with your whole body to throw.

Kenjutsu

Tateki no kurai

Taijutsu

Kenjutsu, continued

Tateki no kurai, continued

Taijutsu, continued

4. *Katatedori ryotemochi—Iriminage ura*
Two-hands-on-one grab—Entering throw (behind)

STRUCTURE △ ○ △
Awase shinogi to *nagare kukuri menuchi sabaki.*

KENJUTSU

As your partner swings up to strike *shomen uchi,* enter with your *ken* positioned in front of you until you are locked together with your partner's *ken* near the area where the *tsuba* or sword guard would be found. Push over the top of your partner's *ken* as if you were striking flint to stone, forcing his *kissaki* away from you back behind him to his right. At the same time move out to the right with *awase shinogi.* As he swings up again enter, sliding in right foot forward, and touch the *kissaki* of your *ken* to your partner's right wrist. Pushing in a circular direction, *tenkan* to the left as your partner also *tenkans* to regain position. Face to face again, your partner swings up for his third strike. Open to the right, and strike *shomen uchi* to complete *nagare kukuri menuchi sabaki.*

TAIJUTSU

You initiate contact by first striking *shomen uchi* with your right hand. Your partner blocks this strike with his right hand and guides your hand downward where he can grab your wrist with both hands. Swing your arm upward in an arc clockwise as your partner continues to grab. Slide in right foot forward, and *tenkan* to the left, guiding your partner with a firm grasp of his neck or shoulder with your left hand. As your partner tries to regain his balance by standing, take one more step forward with your right foot and enter with your whole body to throw.

Practice Points

Beginning students often ask why the first *taijutsu* movement we study begins with a *shomen uchi* strike. Their observation is correct that this kind of strike does not seem practical and is not seen very often in other martial arts. We practice the open hand *shomen uchi* strike because of its relationship with the *shomen uchi* strike used in *kenjutsu.* To initiate a grab from your partner by using the upward swing motion of a *shomen uchi* strike is called *sasoe waza. Sasoe* means "to entice," and *waza* translates as "techniques." To think that Aikido is only a defensive art is to deny the offensive side of Aikido. *Sasoe waza* is a good example of Aikido's offensive side. This type of technique was used frequently by the founder, Morihei Ueshiba, and can be seen in old footage of his demonstrations.

Kenjutsu   *Taijutsu*

Kenjutsu, continued   *Taijutsu, continued*

5. *Mune tsuki* —*Iriminage ura*
High chest punch—Entering throw (behind)

STRUCTURE △ ○ △

Uchi otoshi shinogi to *nagare kukuri menuchi sabaki.*

KENJUTSU

As your partner *tsukis* high, open to the right and counter with *uchi otoshi shinogi*. As he swings up for a second strike, enter sliding in right foot forward and touch your *kissaki* to your partner's right wrist. Pushing in a circular direction, *tenkan* to the left, as your partner also *tenkans* to regain position. Face to face again, your partner swings up for his third strike. Open to the right and as he strikes downward, strike *shomen uchi* to complete *nagare kukuri menuchi sabaki.*

TAIJUTSU

As your partner punches high to your chest, open to the right, and using the blade of your right hand block over your partner's forearm and grab his wrist. Take your partner's balance by extending downward on his wrist and rocking backward slightly. As he tries to right his balance, swing his arm upward in an arc clockwise. Slide in right foot forward, and *tenkan* to the left, guiding your partner with a firm grasp of his neck or shoulder with your left hand. As your partner tries to regain his balance again by standing, take one more step forward with your right foot, and enter with your whole body to throw.

Practice Points

Sometimes when we practice *kenjutsu* the word *tsuki* is translated to mean "poke." Actually, when you *tsuki*, you are not literally trying to poke or skewer your partner. If you actually managed to skewer an opponent during rigorous battle, his last attempts to resist this mortal wound would amount would result in the loss of your sword (at least temporarily) during his struggle. Instead, *tsuki* refers to a cut made as you push forward with your *ken*, most commonly to cut a main artery in the neck. There are traditional schools of *kenjutsu* that do utilize a skewer technique with a long sword; however, the sword is intentionally left in place in the opponent's body and a *wakizashi* (short sword) is used to continue the technique. In *taijutsu*, a *tsuki* is not meant to be a punch to the stomach, but instead a punch to the sternum. For this reason in the most traditional of Aikido books, *tsuki* is referred to as *mune tsuki.*

Kenjutsu

Taijutsu

Kenjutsu, continued   *Taijutsu, continued*

6. *Yokomen uchi—Iriminage ura*
Side strike—Entering throw (behind)

STRUCTURE △ △ ○ △

Awase shinogi to *kaburi shinogi* to *nagare kukuri menuchi sabaki.*

KENJUTSU

As your partner strikes *yokomen uchi*, match his movements as you open to the right with *awase shinogi*. Your partner follows directly with a *tsuki*. Move out to the left and cover with *kaburi shinogi*. As your partner swings up again for a second *yokomen uchi* strike, match his movements again with *awase shinogi*. Pushing in a circular direction, *tenkan* to the left, as your partner also *tenkans* to regain position. Face to face again, your partner swings up for his third strike. Open to the right and as he strikes downward, strike *shomen uchi* to complete *nagare kukuri menuchi sabaki.*

TATEKI NO KURAI

Your first partner strikes *yokomen uchi* from the front as your second partner strikes *shomen uchi* from behind. Match your first partner's movements with *awase shinogi* as you open to the right. Your first partner follows with a *tsuki*, while your second partner strikes *shomen uchi*. Move out to the left with *kaburi shinogi* in response to your first partner's *tsuki*. As both partners swing up again to strike, match your first partner's *yokomen uchi* strike and *tenkan*. Your first partner also *tenkans* for position. Face to face with both partners, your second partner swings up again to strike. Open to the right and as he strikes downward, strike *shomen uchi* to complete *nagare kukuri menuchi sabaki.*

TAIJUTSU

As your partner strikes *yokomen uchi* with his right hand, match his movements, opening to the right as you guide his right hand downward in front of you with your left hand. Move out to the left and guide your partner's arm upward in an arc clockwise with your right hand underneath. Slide in right foot forward, and *tenkan* to the left, guiding your partner with a firm grasp of his neck or shoulder with your left hand. As your partner tries to regain his balance by standing, take one more step forward with your right foot and enter with your whole body to throw.

Kenjutsu	*Tateki no kurai*	*Taijutsu*

Kenjutsu, continued

Tateki no kurai, continued

Taijutsu, continued

7. Ushiro ryotekubidori—Iriminage ura
Behind-both-wrists grab—Entering throw (behind)

STRUCTURE ○ ○ △

No initial *shinogi* movement, beginning directly with *nukidomen sabaki* to *nagare kukuri menuchi sabaki*.

KENJUTSU

As your partner strikes *shomen uchi*, slide to the right with *nukidomen sabaki*. Your partner *tenkans* as you pivot. Face to face again, your partner *tsukis*. Sliding in right foot forward, *tenkan* to the left. Your partner swings up for his third strike. Open to the right and as he strikes downward, strike *shomen uchi* to complete *nagare kukuri menuchi sabaki*.

TATEKI NO KURAI

Both partners strike *shomen uchi*. Slide to the right of your first partner with *nukidomen sabaki*. Your second partner *tsukis*. Slide to the left of your second partner and block his *tsuki* from the outside. *Tenkan* to the left as your second partner also *tenkans*. Open to the right and strike *shomen uchi* to complete *nagare kukuri menuchi sabaki*.

TAIJUTSU

Your partner grabs your left hand then your right as you step under his arm and *tenkan* to the right. Slide in right foot forward and *tenkan* to the left, guiding your partner with a firm grasp of his neck. Take one more step forward with your right foot and enter to throw.

Kenjutsu, continued

Tateki no kurai, continued

Taijutsu, continued

Tenchinage
Sky and ground throw

1. Ryotedori—Tenchinage omote
Both-hands grab—Sky and ground throw (front)

STRUCTURE ☐
Sumi shinogi to *omote kukuri otoshi sabaki.*

KENJUTSU

From a close distance, your partner swings up to strike at your right leg. *Tsuki* toward his face as a feint, then open to the right and block with *sumi shinogi*. As he swings up again for a second strike, slide in right foot forward, touching your *kissaki* to his right wrist. Continue to slide at an angle in front of your partner, using your *ken* to push him forward, forcing his *ken* to the mat with *omote kukuri otoshi sabaki*. After your partner has been immobilized, finish with a left knee or kick to the ribs or take one more step inward with your left foot for a body block.

TAIJUTSU

As your partner reaches toward you with both hands from a close distance, extend your hands toward him as you open to the right with your right foot forward. Use a slight rocking motion to take his balance as you slide forward but at an angle outward as you enter to the right of your partner's left foot. Step inward behind him with your left foot to throw. Done correctly, the footwork completes the zigzag pattern symbolized by the ☐ .

Practice Points

Tenchinage is referred to as the "sky and ground throw" because as you throw, one hand is extended upward, while the other hand extends toward the mat. Good extension in your arms is critical to keep your partner from reversing the technique as you enter. For all Aikido techniques, it is very important to extend your arms and hands. As an extension exercise, have your partner grab your wrist loosely. See if your partner can feel the difference in power as you alternate between having your hand relaxed, extended, and closed tightly in a fist. The extended hand is the most powerful of the three, and your partner should be able to feel that in your wrist. The power generated in Aikido is derived from movements that are expanding and extended in nature, rather than movements that are collapsed or contracting. This is what underlies what some call *kiryoku* or *kokyuryoku* ("ki power").

Kenjutsu

Taijutsu

2. Ryotedori—Tenchinage ura
Both-hands grab—Sky and ground throw (behind)

STRUCTURE ○ □

Uchi otoshi shinogi to *omote kukuri otoshi sabaki.*

KENJUTSU

From a wide distance, your partner *tsukis.* With a big step, slide and enter as you open to the right with *uchi otoshi shinogi.* Deflecting your partner's *ken, tenkan* to the right. Your partner also *tenkans* to regain position. Face to face again, your partner swings up to strike *shomen uchi.* Slide in right foot forward, touching your *kissaki* to his right wrist. Continue to slide at an angle in front of your partner, using your *ken* to push him forward, forcing his *ken* to the mat with *omote kukuri otoshi sabaki.* After your partner has been immobilized, finish with a left knee or kick to the ribs, or take one more step inward with your left foot for a body block.

TATEKI NO KURAI

As your first partner *tsukis* from the front, your second partner strikes *shomen uchi* from behind. Counter your first partner's *tsuki* with *uchi otoshi shinogi* and *tenkan* to the right. Your first partner also *tenkans* for position. Face to face again with both partners, your second partner swings up for a second strike. Slide in right foot forward, touching your *kissaki* to his right wrist. Continue to slide at an angle in front of your second partner, using your *ken* to push him forward, forcing his *ken* to the mat with *omote kukuri otoshi sabaki.* Finish with a left knee or kick to the ribs, or take one more step inward with your left foot for a body block. In this position your second partner acts as a barrier between you and your first partner.

TAIJUTSU

From a wide distance, your partner reaches to grab both of your hands. Extend your hands toward him, open to the right, and lead him into a wide *tenkan.* As your partner tries to regain his balance lost in the momentum of the turn, slide forward but at an angle as you enter to the right of your partner's left foot. Follow with a step inward behind him with your left foot to throw, completing the "zigzag" footwork.

Practice Points

For all Aikido techniques, your posture at the end is just as important as during the execution of a technique. In both *kenjutsu* and *taijutsu* hold your ending posture for a few seconds after completing the technique. Holding your extension and focus after the completion of a technique is called *zanshin.* There are many examples of *zanshin* in our daily lives. For example, when you hit a golf ball, you hold your position and remain focused on the ball until after it has hit the ground and come to a stop. The same holds true when bowling—you remain fixed until the ball has struck the pins. This is also *zanshin.*

Kenjutsu

Tateki no kurai

Taijutsu

Kenjutsu, continued   *Tateki no kurai, continued*   *Taijutsu, continued*

Kaitennage
Rolling throw

1. *Gyaku hanmi katatedori*—*Kaitennage omote*
Opposite-hand grab—Rolling throw (front)

STRUCTURE ○

No initial *shinogi* movement, beginning directly with *nukidomen sabaki*.

KENJUTSU

As your partner swings up to strike *shomen uchi,* slide to the left of your partner, left foot forward. Cut under her right armpit as you step, pivot, and strike downward together with *nukidomen sabaki.*

TAIJUTSU

As your partner grabs your left hand with her right, slide to the left of your partner, left foot forward, step, and pivot under her arm. From your adjusted position guide your partner into a forward roll by casting your arm forward as she holds onto your wrist.

Practice Points

The Japanese word *kaiten* translates in English to mean "one revolution" (as in a circle). This circular motion is not limited to a horizontal plane, but pertains to any angle and dimension in a sphere. This kind of circular motion is inherent in the movement we use when practicing Aikido.

When introducing techniques that include forward rolls to beginning students, this technique allows you to guide your partner into a roll while still giving them the opportunity to let go at any time, if necessary.

Kenjutsu

Taijutsu

2. *Shomen uchi—Kaitennage ura*
Frontal strike—Rolling throw (behind)

STRUCTURE ○ ○

No initial *shinogi* movement, beginning directly with *nagare kukuri sabaki* to *nukidomen sabaki*.

KENJUTSU

From a wide distance, your partner swings up to strike *shomen uchi*. Enter, sliding in right foot forward, and touch your *kissaki* to your partner's right wrist. Pushing in a circular direction, *tenkan* to the left with *nagare kukuri sabaki* to avoid a strike to your right leg, as your partner also *tenkans* for position. Face to face again, your partner swings up for her second strike. Slide across in front of her, left foot forward, cutting under her right armpit as you step, and pivot, striking downward together with *nukidomen sabaki*.

TATEKI NO KURAI

Both partners swing up to strike *shomen uchi* from the front and from behind. Slide forward to avoid the strike from your second partner and touch your *kissaki* to your first partner's right wrist. Pushing in a circular direction, *tenkan* to the left with *nagare kukuri sabaki*, as your first partner also *tenkans* to regain position. Once again face to face, both partners swing up for a second strike. Slide across in front of your first partner, left foot forward, cutting under her right armpit as you step, and pivot, striking downward together with *nukidomen sabaki*.

TAIJUTSU

As your partner strikes *shomen uchi* with her right hand, raise both arms for protection and *tenkan* to the left. Grab over your partner's wrist with your left hand and open, leading your partner around in a circular motion until you are once again face to face. Slide under her arm, left foot forward, step, and pivot. Guide your partner by casting your arm forward, letting go of her hand so that she may move into a forward roll.

Kenjutsu

Tateteki no kurai

Taijutsu

Kenjutsu, continued

Tateki no kurai, continued

Taijutsu, continued

Jujinage
Crossed-arm throw

1. *Katatedori ryotemochi—Jujinage omote*
Two-hands-on-one grab—Crossed-arm throw (front)

STRUCTURE △ □

Awase shinogi to *omote kukuri otoshi sabaki*.

KENJUTSU

As your partner swings up to strike *shomen uchi*, enter with your *ken* positioned in front of you until you are locked together with your partner's *ken* at the area where the *tsuba* or sword guard would be found. Utilizing his momentum, push over the top of your partner's *ken*, forcing his *kissaki* away from you, back behind him to his right, with *awase shinogi*. At the same time, open slightly to the right. As your partner swings up for a second strike, slide in with a forward cut to his right wrist and follow with *omote kukuri otoshi sabaki* until his *ken* is forced to the mat. Finish with a left knee or kick to the ribs, or take one more step with your left foot for a body block.

TAIJUTSU

You initiate contact by first striking *shomen uchi* with your right hand. Your partner blocks this strike with his right hand and guides your hand downward in front of his center where he can grab your wrist with both hands. Extending your right hand, swing your arm upward in a clockwise arc as you open to the right. At the top of the arc, peel off your partner's left hand and cross his arms in front of him above the elbows. Rotate your partner's arms to take his balance, and step in with your left foot. Use your whole body momentum to throw.

Practice Points

Until about 1967, this technique was described in Aikido reference books as *jujigarame*. Recently, this technique has come to be referred to as *jujinage*. The Japanese character for the numeral ten is *ju*, and when it is written it resembles the shape of a cross. This technique was named *jujigarame* or *jujinage* because of the resemblance between your partner's arms once you have crossed them in front of him and the actual shape of a cross. Other Aikido techniques are also named after shapes they resemble. For example, *tembinnage* received its name because the position your partner assumes as you perform this technique resembles a *tembin*—a balance or a scale. Techniques such as *shihonage* and *iriminage* derive their names from descriptions of movements made by *nage* instead of *uke*.

Kenjutsu   *Taijutsu*

Kenjutsu

Taijutsu

2. *Katatedori ryotemochi—Jujinage ura*
Two-hands-on-one grab—Crossed-arm throw (behind)

STRUCTURE △ ○ □

Awase shinogi to *uchi otoshi shinogi* to *omote kukuri otoshi sabaki.*

KENJUTSU

As your partner swings up to strike *shomen uchi*, enter with your *ken* positioned in front of you until you are locked together with your partner's *ken* at the area where the *tsuba* would be. Utilizing his momentum, push over the top of your partner's *ken*, forcing his *kissaki* back behind him to his right with *awase shinogi*. At the same time, open to the right. As your partner *tsukis*, *tenkan* to the right as you counter with *uchi otoshi shinogi*. Your partner also *tenkans*, as you both position yourselves face to face. As your partner swings up again for a third strike, slide in with a forward cut to his right wrist and follow with *omote kukuri otoshi sabaki* until his *ken* is forced to the mat.

TATEKI NO KURAI

As both partners swing up to strike *shomen uchi*, enter with your *ken* positioned in front of you until you are locked together with your first partner's *ken*. Utilizing his momentum, push over the top of his *ken*, forcing his *kissaki* back behind him to his right with *awase shinogi*. *Tenkan* to the right as you counter your first partner's *tsuki* with *uchi otoshi shinogi*. Face to face again, both partners strike *shomen uchi*. Your second partner is the closest to you, therefore, enter toward him with a forward cut to his right wrist and follow with *omote kukuri otoshi sabaki*.

TAIJUTSU

You begin by striking *shomen uchi* with your right hand. Your partner blocks this strike with his right hand and guides your hand downward in front of his center, where he can grab your wrist with both hands. Extending your right hand, swing your arm upward in a circular motion as you *tenkan* to the right. Lead your partner in a circular direction until you are face to face. Peel off your partner's left hand and cross his arms in front of him above the elbows. Rotate your partner's arms to take his balance, and step in with your left foot. Use your whole body to throw.

Kenjutsu　　　　　*Tateki no kurai*　　　　　*Taijutsu*

Kenjutsu, continued

Tateki no kurai, continued

Taijutsu, continued

3. Ryotedori—Jujinage omote
Both-hands grab—Crossed-arm throw (front)

STRUCTURE △ ○

Waki shinogi to *omote kukuri otoshi sabaki.*

KENJUTSU

As your partner swings up to strike *shomen uchi, tsuki* toward his face as a feint to distract him. As he strikes downward, open to the right with *waki shinogi.* As your partner swings up for a second strike, match his movement, sliding in right foot forward with a forward cut to his right wrist. Follow with *omote kukuri otoshi sabaki* until his *ken* is forced to the mat. Finish with a left knee or kick to the ribs, or take one more step with your left foot for a body block.

TAIJUTSU

As your partner approaches to grab, extend both of your hands toward him as you open to the right. As he reaches for your left hand with his right, grab over his right hand and peel it off with your right hand. Using your free left hand, grab your partner's left wrist from underneath and cross his arms in front of him above the elbows. Rotate your partner's arms to take his balance, and step in with your right foot. Use your whole body momentum to throw.

Practice Points

To execute this technique, it is important to use large movements to cross your partner's arms correctly above the elbows in front of him. Once your partner's arms are crossed, take one more step in to throw. *Jujinage* can be completed with a *koshinage* or *kokyunage* throw, but for general practice it is safer to rotate your partner's crossed arms to take his balance and extend him into a back roll. Release his hands quickly once he has begun to fall. By releasing his hands quickly he can use his arms to protect himself as he falls.

Kenjutsu

Taijutsu

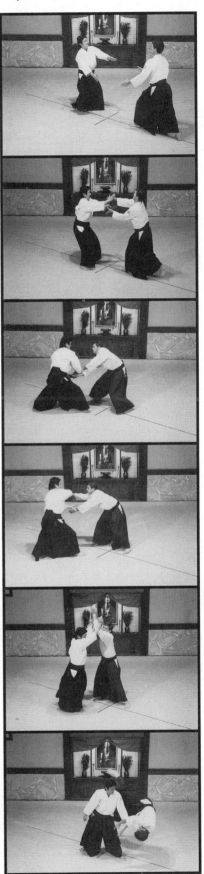

Koshinage
Hip throw

1. *Shomen uchi—Koshinage*
   Frontal strike—Hip throw

STRUCTURE △ ○
Waki shinogi to *nukidomen sabaki.*

KENJUTSU

As your partner swings up to strike *shomen uchi, tsuki* toward his face to distract him. As he strikes downward, open to the right with *waki shinogi.* As he swings up again, enter, left foot forward, and cut upward with your *ken.* Cut from your partner's groin upward through his chest and collarbone area. As he strikes downward, pivot and strike downward with *nukidomen sabaki.* As you are cutting upward, the distance between you and your partner is important. If you are too close you will not be able to execute this movement.

TATEKI NO KURAI

As both partners swing up to strike *shomen uchi, tsuki* toward your first partner's face to distract him. As they strike downward, open to the right with *waki shinogi* to avoid both strikes. As both partners swing up again for a second strike, enter with your left foot forward toward your first partner and cut upward with your *ken.* Pivot, and strike downward in the direction of your second partner with *nukidomen sabaki.*

TAIJUTSU

As your partner strikes *shomen uchi* with his right hand, open to the right as you guide your partner's striking hand downward toward your center with your right hand underneath his and your left hand crossed on top. Breaking his balance, extend your partner's arm in front of you as you start to slide across in front of him, right foot forward (as if you were going to do *shihonage*). As your partner rights himself to regain his balance, use the momentum of his shifting weight to lift his arm upward with your right hand. Step in and squat low on your left leg, load your partner over the back of your hips, and throw by straightening your leg as you rock your partner forward. Finish the throw by tucking in your right hand and foot.

Practice Points
Koshinage, or hip throws, require the use of your partner's momentum to execute. Timing is very important. When you raise your partner's arm upward, keep your arm straight and vertical and focus your eyes upward toward your hand in the air. Do not bend your elbow. As your partner starts to fall, draw your throwing arm toward your center. For your protection, make sure to also pull in your extended leg as you throw so that your partner does not land on it when he falls.

Kenjutsu

Tateki no kurai

Taijutsu

Kenjutsu, continued

Tateki no kurai, continued

Taijutsu, continued

2. Yokomen uchi—Koshinage
Side strike—Hip throw

STRUCTURE △ ○

Awase shinogi to *uchi otoshi shinogi* to *nukidomen sabaki.*

KENJUTSU

As your partner strikes *yokomen uchi,* match his movements and block with *awase shinogi* as you open to the right. As your partner follows directly with a *tsuki,* block his movement with *uchi otoshi shinogi,* deflecting his *ken* back behind him as you open again slightly to the right. As he swings up again to strike *shomen uchi,* enter left foot forward, and cut upward with your *ken.* As he strikes downward, pivot and strike downward in the same direction with *nukidomen sabaki.*

TAIJUTSU

As your partner strikes *yokomen uchi* with his right hand, open to the right as you guide his striking hand with your left hand downward toward your center. Breaking his balance, extend your partner's arm in front of you as you start to slide across in front of him, right foot forward. As he rights himself to regain his balance, use the momentum of his shifting weight to lift his arm upward with your right hand. Step in and squat low on your left leg. Load your partner over the back of your hips and throw by straightening your leg as you rock your partner forward. Finish the throw by tucking in your right hand and foot.

> **Practice Points**
> When first practicing hip throws, it is important that both partners cooperate fully with each other, offering no resistance. When throwing your partner, it is better not to kneel on one knee, as this will bring your partner's head too close to the mat as he is thrown over. If working with a partner who is not quite advanced enough to practice this *ukemi,* do the technique until your partner is completely loaded onto the back of your hips, then lower them back gently to the mat. Pay attention to safety, as this is an advanced technique.

Kenjutsu   *Taijutsu*

Kenjutsu, continued   *Taijutsu, continued*

3. Tsuki—Koshinage
Punch—Hip throw

STRUCTURE ○ ○

No initial *shinogi* movement, beginning directly with *nagare kukuri sabaki* to *nukidomen sabaki*.

KENJUTSU

From a wide distance your partner *tsukis*. Block over your partner's *ken* from the left as you *tenkan* to the left with *nagare kukuri sabaki*. Your partner also *tenkans* to reposition himself face to face. As he swings up again to strike, enter right foot forward, and cut upward with your *ken*. As he strikes downward, pivot and strike downward in the same direction with *nukidomen sabaki*.

TAIJUTSU

As your partner *tsukis* with his right hand, swing both of your arms upward as you *tenkan* to the left. As you complete the *tenkan*, grab over your partner's striking hand with your left hand and lead him around in a circular motion until you are again face to face. Keeping a hold of your partner's right hand with your left, raise his arm high and use your right hand and arm as a brace under his upper arm to lift him as you step in with your right foot. Load your partner over the back of your hips and throw by straightening your legs as you rock your partner forward.

Practice Points

Many *nage waza* like *iriminage* and *shihonage*, for example, can incorporate *koshinage* as an ending. *Katame waza* (joint locking techniques) such as *kote gaeshi* can also incorporate *koshinage* as an ending. Therefore, *koshinage* is not considered only as an independent technique. It is also considered as *ouyo waza* (applied techniques) where one technique is compounded with another.

Kenjutsu   *Taijutsu*

Kenjutsu, continued   *Taijutsu, continued*

4. *Ushiro ryotekubidori—Koshinage*
Behind-both-wrists grab—Hip throw

STRUCTURE △ △ ○ ○

Awase shinogi to *waki shinogi* to *nukidomen sabaki* to *nukidomen sabaki.*

KENJUTSU

As your partner swings up to strike *shomen uchi*, slide in, blocking his *ken* from the left with *awase shinogi*. Force his *ken* back behind him to his left, as you open to the left again with *waki shinogi*. As he swings up again, slide to the left of your partner, left foot forward, cutting under his right armpit as you step, pivot, and strike downward with *nukidomen sabaki*. Your partner *tenkans* to regain position. Face to face, he swings up for his third strike. Enter left foot forward, cutting upward with your *ken*. Step, pivot, and cut downward for *nukidomen sabaki*.

TATEKI NO KURAI

As both partners swing up to strike *shomen uchi*, focus on your first partner and block his *ken* from the left with *awase shinogi*. Force his *ken* back behind him to his left, and open to the left again with *waki shinogi*. As both partners swing up again, slide to the left of your first partner, left foot forward, cutting under his right armpit as you step, pivot, and strike downward for *nukidomen sabaki*. Face to face, both partners swing up again. Enter toward your first partner, left foot forward, cutting upward with your *ken*. Step, pivot, and cut downward for *nukidomen sabaki*.

TAIJUTSU

You initiate contact by striking *shomen uchi* with your right hand. Your partner blocks this strike with his right hand and guides your hand downward in front of his center to grab. Palm up, slide to the left of your partner, and *tenkan* under his raised arm. As he turns to grab your free left hand, grab his left hand first and raise his arm over your head as you step in and squat low on your right leg. Load your partner over the back of your hips and throw by straightening your leg as you rock your partner forward. Finish the throw by tucking in your left hand and foot. (This *nukidomen sabaki* relationship to *koshinage* is a slight variation of the standard *nukidomen sabaki*.)

Kenjutsu	Tateki no kurai	Taijutsu

Kenjutsu, continued

Tateki no kurai, continued

Taijutsu, continued

Kokyunage
Timing throw

1. *Aihanmi katatedori—Kokyunage*
Same-hand grab—Timing throw

STRUCTURE △ ○
Waki shinogi to *nukidomen sabaki*.

KENJUTSU

As your partner swings up to strike *shomen uchi, tsuki* toward his face as a feint to distract him. As he strikes downward, open to the right with *waki shinogi*. As he swings up again to strike, slide across in front of your partner, right foot forward, cutting low to high under his left armpit as you step, pivot, and strike downward to complete *nukidomen sabaki*.

TAIJUTSU

From a wide distance, lead your partner as he grabs your right hand with his right hand, and open to the right, taking his balance. Hand extended, swing your partner's arm upward in an arc clockwise. Using your left hand as a brace under his elbow, slide in front of your partner, right foot forward, and *tenkan* under his arm. Now facing the opposite direction, extend your partner's arm using his grip on your wrist as an anchor and throw by taking one more step, right foot forward, with your free hand bracing the inside of his elbow.

> **Practice Points**
> *Kokyunage* is also called *aikinage*, which translates in English as "timing throw." The extent and definition of this category of techniques are somewhat vague. The principle can be generally characterized as techniques that utilize throws executed without grabbing one's partner. In actuality, however, sometimes we do grab our partner's arm or uniform to ensure the throw will be completed in the event that our partner lets go of his or her grab. This technique is a good example.

Kenjutsu

Taijutsu

Kenjutsu, continued

Taijutsu, continued

2. *Gyaku hanmi katatedori—Kokyunage*
Opposite-hand grab—Timing throw

STRUCTURE △ □

Sumi shinogi to *omote kukuri otoshi sabaki.*

KENJUTSU

As your partner strikes low to your right leg, slide forward and, opening to the right, block with *sumi shinogi*. As he swings up for a second strike, slide in right foot forward, cutting forward with your *kissaki* to your partner's right wrist. Continue to slide, right foot forward, in front of your partner, using your *ken* to push him forward, forcing his *ken* to the mat with *omote kukuri otoshi sabaki*. After your partner has been immobilized, take one more step with your left foot and hold.

TAIJUTSU

From a close distance, your partner grabs your right hand with his right hand. Slide in, right foot forward, at an angle to the right away from your partner, breaking his balance. Take one more step in with your left foot at an angle toward him, and throw with your free hand bracing the inside of his elbow.

> **Practice Points**
> Variations of this technique can be achieved by adding movements with your free hand during the beginning of the technique. If you extend your free hand across your partner's chest and neck, the technique becomes *tenchinage*, or *iriminage*. If you push his chin backward with your palm extended outward, the technique becomes *ago ate*. These names vary depending on the instructor. If your partner offers resistance, this technique can be changed to *koshinage*. If your partner is coming at a higher rate of speed from a wider distance, an opening move can be added to accommodate the increase in velocity.

Kenjutsu

Taijutsu

Kenjutsu, continued   *Taijutsu, continued*

3. Shomen uchi—Kokyunage
Frontal strike—Timing throw

STRUCTURE △ ○

Awase shinogi to *nukidomen sabaki.*

KENJUTSU

As your partner swings up, match his movements. As he strikes downward, open to the right with *awase shinogi.* As he swings up for a second strike, enter left foot forward, and cut upward with your *ken.* Cut from your partner's groin upward through his chest and collarbone area. As he strikes downward, pivot and strike downward in the same direction to complete *nukidomen sabaki.*

TATEKI NO KURAI

As both partners swing up to strike *shomen uchi* from the front and from behind, match their movement. As they strike downward, open to the right with *awase shinogi* avoiding both strikes. As both partners swing up again for a second strike, enter with your left foot forward toward your first partner, and cut upward with your *ken.* Step, pivot, and strike downward in the direction of your second partner to complete *nukidomen sabaki.*

TAIJUTSU

As your partner strikes *shomen uchi* with his right hand, open to the right as you grab over the top of his hand with your right hand. Extend him forward slightly to take his balance. Raise his arm upward in an arc clockwise. Slide across the front of your partner, right foot forward, with your left hand under his elbow as as brace, and *tenkan.* Facing the opposite direction, extend your partner's arm using your grip on his wrist as an anchor and throw by taking one more step with your free hand bracing the inside of his elbow.

Practice Points
This technique is useful when practicing arm hold techniques with an *uke* who offers resistance as you attempt to rotate his arm forward. If you meet resistance at the top of the arc, adjust and *tenkan* under his raised arm. Use his resistance to throw from the other direction. If your partner still offers resistance as you attempt to throw, you can change the technique to *shihonage, kote gaeshi,* or *iriminage* from this position. As you move under your partner's raised arm, your partner has a chance to punch you in the face. There is a series of techniques to deal with this as well.

Kenjutsu

Tateki no kurai

Taijutsu

Kenjutsu, continued

Tateki no kurai, continued

Taijutsu, continued

4. *Yokomen uchi—Kokyunage* #1
Side strike—Timing throw #1

STRUCTURE △ △

Awase shinogi to *uchi otoshi shinogi.*

KENJUTSU

As your partner strikes *yokomen uchi,* match his movements with *awase shinogi* as you open to the right. As your partner follows directly with a *tsuki,* block his movement with *uchi otoshi shinogi,* pushing his *ken* back behind him to his right, as you open again slightly to the right. As your partner swings up again to strike *shomen uchi,* enter in low, right foot forward. From underneath point your *kissaki* upward toward his abdomen.

TAIJUTSU

As your partner strikes *yokomen uchi* with his right hand, open to the right and guide his striking hand with your left hand downward toward your center to grab with both hands. Extend his arm forward past his center to take his balance. As he rights himself, raise his arm upward with your right hand and enter, lowering yourself to one knee. Throw your partner over your right shoulder.

> **Practice Points**
> This is an example of *shihonage henka waza. Henka waza* are techniques that begin as one technique and are changed by *nage* into another during the course of the technique. When practicing *kenjutsu,* enter in as low and close as possible to avoid a strike. Plant the point of your sword into your partner's abdomen from underneath. In an actual battle between samurai, one would abandon his sword, leaving it in place in his enemy's belly as he escaped. For *taijutsu,* take your partner's balance after capturing his arm and continue to use his momentum as you enter in low with a body block to his legs. As you throw, keep your throwing arm held high and support your partner so that he has enough clearance to complete the fall. Make sure your partner has enough experience to do the correct *ukemi* from this position.

Kenjutsu

Taijutsu

Kenjutsu, continued   *Taijutsu, continued*

5. *Yokomen uchi—Kokyunage* #2
Side strike—Timing throw #2

STRUCTURE ☐
No initial *shinogi* movement, beginning directly with *omote kukuri otoshi sabaki.*

KENJUTSU

As your partner swings up to strike *yokomen uchi* from the left, match his timing carefully and slide in as he swings up. Touch your *kissaki* to his right wrist and cut forward as you slide, right foot forward, in front of your partner using your *ken* to force his *ken* to the mat with *omote kukuri otoshi sabaki.* Take one more step with your left foot and hold.

TAIJUTSU

As your partner swings up to strike *yokomen uchi* with his left hand, enter and slide right foot forward at an angle to the right. Extend both of your arms in front of you as you make contact with your partner's arm. Take one more step at an angle inward to the left behind your partner to throw.

Practice Points

It is fairly standard *ukemi* these days to use break-falls when practicing *kokyunage.* It is important to remember that break-falls are not based in reality and have been created as a choreographed response. To train for the power and positioning used when executing *kokyunage* throws, *kokyu ryoku* is practiced. *Kokyunage* training is important for executing *kuzushi waza* (techniques that initiate by breaking your partner's balance before executing a throw). Proper *kokyunage* training helps you in extending your partners off their center of balance so that other techniques can be applied.

Kenjutsu

Taijutsu

Kenjutsu, continued   *Taijutsu, continued*

6. *Mune tsuki—Kokyunage*
Chest punch—Timing throw

STRUCTURE ○ □
Nagare kukuri sabaki to *omote kukuri otoshi sabaki.*

KENJUTSU

As your partner *tsukis*, block over your partner's *ken* from left to right with *nagare kukuri sabaki*, as you both *tenkan* for position. Face to face again, your partner swings up for a second strike. Slide in, left foot forward, touching your *kissaki* to your partner's left wrist. Extend your partner forward with your *ken*, forcing his *ken* to the mat with *omote kukuri sabaki*. Step in with your right foot and hold.

TAIJUTSU

As your partner *tsukis* high to your chest with his left hand, *tenkan* to the left, grabbing over his right wrist with your left hand. Guide him around in a circular motion until you are once again face to face. Change hands, grabbing your partner's right arm with your left hand near the inside of his elbow, and take one more step with your right foot to throw.

> **Practice Points**
> Keep in mind that even though we practice *kenjutsu* with *bokken*, the movements and the intentions behind them are the same as using actual swords. If you analyze these techniques as they are practiced with a sword made of wood, you will probably experience some concerns as to their effectiveness. For example, one might wonder what would happen if your partner resisted while you were trying to execute *omote kukuri otoshi sabaki*. If using a sword, even a slight touch to the wrist could cause a lot of damage. If you are cutting forward with your *ken* as you extend your partner forward toward the mat, there would be little chance of resistance. During *nagare kukuri sabaki*, as *uke*, the safest way to retreat from your partner as he touches his *ken* to your wrist is to *tenkan*. If using a real *ken*, were you to simply back up, you would open yourself up to additional strikes. The founder, Morihei Ueshiba, used this technique of cutting forward on or just touching the wrist with a *ken* widely. Remember that we use *bokken* for safety reasons, but the techniques are sword techniques. Practice with *bokken* that entails much banging of wood is practiced by those who do not know how to use a real *ken*.

Kenjutsu   *Taijutsu*

Kenjutsu, continued   *Taijutsu, continued*

 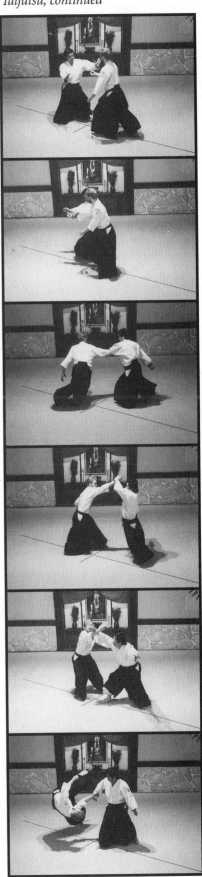

7. *Ryotemochi—Kokyunage*
Both-hands grab—Timing throw

STRUCTURE △

Uchi otoshi shinogi.

KENJUTSU

From a wide distance, as your partner *tsukis,* open to the right with *uchi otoshi shinogi.* As he swings up again, enter low, right foot forward, to the right and cut your partner's thigh.

TAIJUTSU

As your partner approaches to grab from a wide distance, offer both hands to him and open to the right. As you open, lower yourself while raising both arms back behind you. Propel your partner over your head behind you into a forward roll.

Practice Points

In actuality, if you were a samurai practicing *kenjutsu,* you would make a cut to your partner's thigh and escape as soon as possible. Or, you would plant your *ken* in your partner's abdomen from underneath and escape. As a *taijutsu* exercise, this technique is helpful for practicing correct *mawai* and timing. Realistically, your partner would probably kick you in the face instead of doing a forward roll.

Kenjutsu

Taijutsu

Nage Katame Waza
Joint Stimulation Throwing Techniques

Originally, most Aikido throwing techniques included elements of joint stimulation. Today, any Aikido technique can be adapted to include a joint stimulation. *Kote gaeshi* (wrist twist) is the primary example used in this book for throwing techniques that utilize joint stimulations. The *kenjutsu* relationship for techniques that end with *kote gaeshi* is *makiuchi zuki sabaki*. The technique *kote gaeshi* can be completed with either a standing or a floor pin. Since we are concentrating on *kenjutsu–taijutsu* relationships, the pins have been omitted in the following section. For reference, the *kote gaeshi* floor pin was explained on page 48.

Kote gaeshi
Wrist twist

1. Shomen uchi—Kote gaeshi omote
Frontal strike—Wrist twist (front)

STRUCTURE △ △

Awase shinogi to *makiuchi zuki sabaki*.

KENJUTSU

As your partner swings up to strike *shomen uchi*, match his movements. As he strikes downward, open to the left, and block over his *ken* from the left with *awase shinogi*. Your partner follows with an additional *tsuki*. Open to the right, deflecting his *ken* counter-clockwise with a rolling block counter-clockwise from underneath, and touch your *kissaki* to your partner's left wrist to complete *makiuchi zuki sabaki*.

TAIJUTSU

As your partner strikes *shomen uchi* with his right hand, grab over his striking hand with your left hand as you open to the left. Extend your partner forward to take his balance. Cross in front of your partner and open to the right. Twist your partner's wrist to the outside, extending his hand toward his body. Keeping a lock on his wrist, turn and take one more step to throw.

Practice Points

Kote gaeshi is widely translated as "wrist twist." Some take that too literally, however, and tend to rotate their partner's hand and wrist horizontally, pulling their partner's arm away from their body. Actually it is more like a "wrist roll," twisting your partner's wrist so that his fingers point back in toward his arm and body. In traditional *Jujitsu*, this technique is called *kote hineri* and is quite popular. As *nage*, if you do not do this technique properly, you leave yourself open for a round kick from your partner as you cross in front of him.

Kenjutsu

Taijutsu

Kenjutsu, continued

Taijutsu, continued

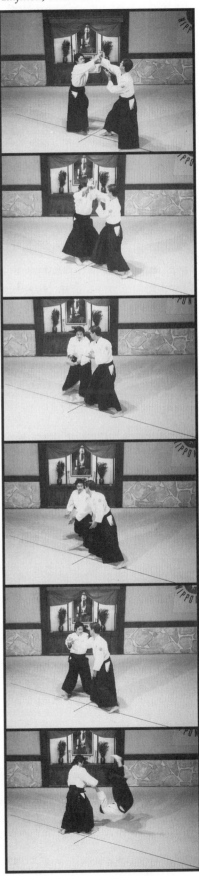

2. *Shomen uchi—Kote gaeshi ura*
Frontal strike—Wrist twist (behind)

STRUCTURE ○ △

No initial *shinogi* movement, beginning directly with *nagare kukuri makiuchi zuki sabaki*.

KENJUTSU

As your partner swings up to strike *shomen uchi,* enter right foot forward and cut forward with your *kissaki* to your partner's right wrist. Pushing in a circular direction with your *ken, tenkan* to the left to avoid a strike to your right leg. Your partner also *tenkans* for position. Face to face again, your partner *tsukis.* Open to the right, deflecting his *tsuki* counter-clockwise with a rolling block. Touch your *kissaki* to your partner's left wrist to complete *nagare kukuri makiuchi zuki sabaki.*

TATEKI NO KURAI

Both partners swing up to strike *shomen uchi.* Enter toward your first partner, right foot forward, and cut forward with your *kissaki* to your partner's right wrist. Pushing in a circular direction, *tenkan* to the left to avoid a strike to your right leg. Your partner also *tenkans* for position. Face to face with both partners, your second partner *tsukis.* Open to the right, deflecting his *tsuki* with a rolling block. Touch your *kissaki* to your second partner's left wrist to complete *nagare kukuri makiuchi zuki sabaki.*

TAIJUTSU

Your partner swings up to strike *shomen uchi* with his right hand. *Tenkan* to the left as you grab over his right wrist with your right hand. Guide your partner in a circular direction until you are face to face and open to the right. Twist his wrist to the outside, extending his hand toward his body. Keeping a lock on his wrist, turn and take one more step to throw.

> **Practice Points**
> We have all seen the results of applying too much force to a wrist twist technique. Wrists are vulnerable areas and take a long time to heal once damaged. Make sure you stretch out your wrists completely during Aikido exercises before practice. Practicing *suburi* individually or practicing *bokken* movements using the *uchiuma* (horse made of branch bundles) are both helpful for strengthening your wrists. Make sure you understand your partner's level of experience, and practice accordingly.

Kenjutsu

Tateki no kurai

Taijutsu

Kenjutsu, continued

Tateki no kurai, continued

Taijutsu, continued

3. *Yokomen uchi—Kote gaeshi omote*
Side strike—Wrist twist (front)

STRUCTURE △ △ △

Awase shinogi to *uchi otoshi shinogi* to *makiuchi zuki sabaki.*

KENJUTSU

As your partner strikes *yokomen uchi*, open to the right and match his movements with *awase shinogi*. As he follows directly with a *tsuki*, open to the right and block with *uchi otoshi shinogi*. As your partner swings up again to strike, open to the right, cutting under his left armpit. For a last strike your partner *tsukis*. Open to the right, deflecting his *tsuki* counter-clockwise with a rolling block. Touch your *kissaki* to your partner's left wrist to complete *makiuchi zuki sabaki.*

TATEKI NO KURAI

Your first partner strikes *yokomen uchi* from the front as your second partner strikes *shomen uchi* from behind. Open to the right with *awase shinogi*, blocking your first partner's strike. Open to the right again with *uchi otoshi shinogi* to block an additional *tsuki* from your first partner. As both partners swing up again, open to the right, cutting under your first partner's armpit. Your first partner *tsukis* again. Open to the right, deflecting his *tsuki* with a rolling block. Touch your *kissaki* to your partner's left wrist to complete *makiuchi zuki sabaki.*

TAIJUTSU

As your partner strikes *yokomen uchi* with his right hand, open to the right as you guide his striking hand downward with your left hand toward your center. Take your partner's balance and open to the right again. Twist your partner's wrist to the outside, extending his hand toward his body. Keeping a lock on his wrist, turn and take one more step to throw.

Kenjutsu   *Tateki no kurai*   *Taijutsu*

Kenjutsu, continued   *Tateki no kurai, continued*   *Taijutsu, continued*

4. *Yokomen uchi—Kote gaeshi ura*
Side strike—Wrist twist (behind)

STRUCTURE △ △ ○ △
Awase shinogi to *kaburi shinogi* to *nagare kukuri makiuchi zuki sabaki.*

KENJUTSU

Open to the right as your partner strikes *yokomen uchi* and block with *awase shinogi.* Against an additional *tsuki,* move out to the left with *kaburi shinogi.* As he swings up again to strike *yokomen uchi,* match his movements as both of you *tenkan.* Face to face again, your partner *tsukis* again. Open to the right, deflecting his *tsuki* with a rolling block. Touch your *kissaki* to your partner's left wrist to complete *nagare kukuri makiuchi zuki sabaki.*

TATEKI NO KURAI

(Refer to *kenjutsu* explanation.)

TAIJUTSU

As your partner strikes *yokomen uchi,* open to the right as you guide his right striking hand downward with your left hand. With your right hand, sweep his striking hand upward in an arc clockwise as you move out to the left. *Tenkan* to the left as you grab over his right wrist. Open to the right, keeping a lock on his wrist. Turn and take one more step to throw.

Kenjutsu	*Tateki no kurai*	*Taijutsu*

Kenjutsu, continued

Tateki no kurai, continued

Taijutsu, continued

5. *Mune tsuki—Kote gaeshi omote*
   Punch—Wrist twist (front)

STRUCTURE △ △
Uchi otoshi shinogi to *makiuchi zuki sabaki*.

KENJUTSU

As your partner *tsukis* from the right, open to the left and block from left to right with *uchi otoshi shinogi*. Without stepping, your partner follows rapidly with another *tsuki* from the left. Open to the right this time, and with a rolling block deflect his *tsuki*. Touch your *kissaki* to your partner's left wrist to complete *makiuchi zuki sabaki*.

TAIJUTSU

Open to the left as your partner punches with his right hand. Deflect the blow with your left hand then grab over his right hand with your left. Open again to the right and twist your partner's wrist with your right hand. Keeping a lock on his wrist, turn and take one more step to throw.

Practice Points
When you deflect your partner's punch, use the blade or edge of your hand between the base of your pinkie and your wrist. Extend your hand and hit down firmly. Try not to focus your concentration only on your partner's fist. Maintain your distance and be aware of his whole body, as another punch or grab could come from his free hand. Also watch for an *atemi* with his knee or a round kick with his opposite foot.

Kenjutsu   *Taijutsu*

Kenjutsu

Taijutsu

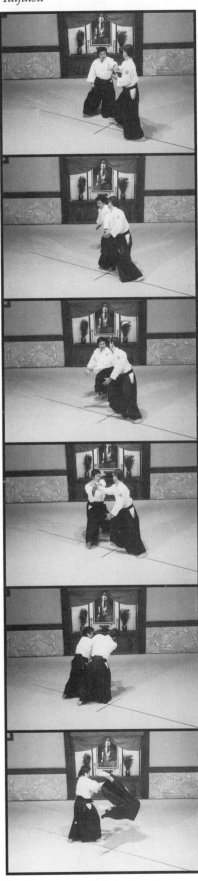

6. *Mune tsuki—Kote gaeshi ura*
Punch—Wrist twist (behind)

STRUCTURE ○ △

No initial *shinogi* movement, beginning directly with *nagare kukuri makiuchi zuki sabaki*.

KENJUTSU

As your partner *tsukis* high, enter right foot forward and cut forward from the left with your *kissaki* to your partner's right wrist. Pushing in a circular direction with your *ken, tenkan* to the left to avoid a strike to your right leg. Your partner also *tenkans* for position. Face to face again, your partner *tsukis*. Open to the right, deflecting his *tsuki* with a rolling block. Touch your *kissaki* to your partner's left wrist to complete *nagare kukuri makiuchi zuki sabaki*.

TATEKI NO KURAI

Your first partner *tsukis* high, as your second partner strikes *shomen uchi* from behind. Slide in right foot forward from the left, toward your first partner, and cut forward with your *kissaki* to your partner's right wrist. *Tenkan* to the left to avoid a strike from behind from your second partner. Your first partner also *tenkans* for position. Face to face again with both partners, your second partner *tsukis*. Open to the right, deflecting his *tsuki* with a rolling block. Touch your *kissaki* to your second partner's left wrist to complete *nagare kukuri makiuchi zuki sabaki*.

TAIJUTSU

As your partner punches high to your chest with his right hand from the left, slide in right foot forward and *tenkan* to the left as you grab over his right wrist. Open to the right as you twist his wrist to the outside, extending his hand toward his body. Keeping a lock on his wrist, turn and take one more step to throw.

> **Practice Points**
> The ending of this technique, *kote gaeshi*, can easily be changed to other techniques such as *ago ate, kokyunage*, or *koshinage*.

Kenjutsu

Tateki no kurai

Taijutsu

Kenjutsu, continued   *Tateki no kurai, continued*   *Taijutsu, continued*

7. *Gyaku hanmi katatedori—Kote gaeshi ura*
Opposite-hand grab—Wrist twist (behind)

STRUCTURE ○ △

Kaburi shinogi to *nagare kukuri makiuchi zuki sabaki.*

KENJUTSU

As your partner swings up to strike *shomen uchi, tsuki* toward his face as a feint to distract him. Move out to the left and cover with *kaburi shinogi,* as he strikes downward. As he swings up for a second strike, enter, right foot forward, and cut forward with your *kissaki* to your partner's right wrist. Pushing in a circular direction with your *ken, tenkan* to the left to avoid a strike to your right leg. Your partner also *tenkans* for position. Face to face again, your partner *tsukis.* Open to the right, deflecting his *tsuki* with a rolling block. Touch your *kissaki* to your partner's left wrist to complete *nagare kukuri makiuchi zuki sabaki.*

TATEKI NO KURAI

As both partners swing up to strike *shomen uchi, tsuki* toward your first partner's face as a feint. Move out to the left and cover with *kaburi shinogi,* avoiding both strikes. As both partners swing up for a second strike, enter right foot forward, and cut forward with your *kissaki* to your partner's right wrist. Pushing in a circular direction with your *ken, tenkan* to the left. Your first partner also *tenkans* for position. Face to face again with both partners, your second partner *tsukis.* Open to the right, deflecting his *tsuki* with a rolling block. Touch your *kissaki* to your second partner's left wrist to complete *nagare kukuri makiuchi zuki sabaki.*

TAIJUTSU

From a wide distance, your partner grabs your left hand with his right. Move out to the left as you bring both of your hands upward, crossed in front of you. Release your wrist from your partner's grip by using your right hand as a brace. Grab over his right hand as you *tenkan* to the left. Open to the right as you twist his wrist to the outside, extending his hand toward his body. Keeping a lock on his wrist, turn and take one more step to throw.

Kenjutsu

Tateki no kurai

Taijutsu

Kenjutsu, continued

Tateki no kurai, continued

Taijutsu, continued

8. *Katatedori ryotemochi*—*Kote gaeshi omote*
Two-hands-on-one grab—Wrist twist (front)

STRUCTURE △ △ △
Waki shinogi to *sumi shinogi* to *makiuchi zuki sabaki.*

KENJUTSU

As your partner swings up to strike *shomen uchi, tsuki* toward her face and open to the right with *waki shinogi.* She follows with a low strike to your right shin. Counter by sliding in, right foot forward, with *sumi shinogi.* As she continues with an additional *tsuki,* open to the right, deflecting her *tsuki* with a rolling block. Touch your *kissaki* to her left wrist to complete *nagare kukuri makiuchi zuki sabaki.*

TAIJUTSU

Your partner approaches from a wide distance. Extend your right hand toward her, palm up. As she grabs your hand with both hands, open to the right. Open to the right again, grabbing your partner's right wrist with your left hand. Twist her wrist to the outside, extending her hand toward her body. Keeping a lock on her wrist, turn and take one more step to throw.

Practice Points
Top photo: If you extend your partner's arm away from his body as you twist his wrist, you can open yourself up for a high round kick to the head or a knee to the ribs as shown in top photo.
Middle and bottom photos: Extending your partner's arm toward his body is correct. From this position, even if your partner resists and tucks his arm tight against his body, you have the opportunity to use a knee to his ribs (middle photo), or to change the technique to *ago ate,* or a leg sweep, for example (bottom photo).

Kenjutsu

Taijutsu

9. *Katatedori ryotemochi—Kote gaeshi ura*
Two-hands-on-one grab—Wrist twist (behind)

STRUCTURE △ ○ △
Uchi otoshi shinogi to *nagare kukuri makiuchi zuki sabaki.*

KENJUTSU

As your partner *tsukis,* open to the right with *uchi otoshi shinogi.* As she swings up for a second strike, slide in cutting forward to her right wrist as both of you *tenkan.* Face to face again, open to the right, deflecting an additional *tsuki* with a rolling block. Touch your *kissaki* to her left wrist to complete *nagare kukuri makiuchi zuki sabaki.*

TATEKI NO KURAI

Your first partner *tsukis* as your second partner strikes *shomen uchi* from behind. Open to the right with *uchi otoshi shinogi* to avoid both strikes. Both partners swing up for a second strike. Enter toward your first partner and cut forward to her right wrist as both of you *tenkan.* Face to face again with both partners, open to the right, deflecting an additional *tsuki* from your second partner with a rolling block. Touch your *kissaki* to your second partner's left wrist to complete *nagare kukuri makiuchi zuki sabaki.*

TAIJUTSU

Extend your right hand toward your partner palm down, as she approaches to grab with both hands. Open to the right as you swing your arm upward in an arc clockwise, breaking her grip. Grab over her right hand as you *tenkan.* Open to the right as you twist her wrist to the outside, extending her hand toward her body. Keeping a lock on her wrist, turn and take one more step to throw.

Kenjutsu

Tateki no kurai

Taijutsu

Kenjutsu, continued

Tateki no kurai, continued

Taijutsu, continued

10. Katadori shomen uchi—Kote gaeshi omote
One-hand shoulder grab—Frontal strike (front)

STRUCTURE △ △
Awase shinogi to *makiuchi zuki sabaki.*

KENJUTSU
From a close distance, match your partner's movement as she swings up to strike *shomen uchi*. With *kens* locked, push and release, opening to the right with *awase shinogi*, forcing her *ken* back behind her to her right. As she swings up for a second strike, open to the right, cutting across to her left armpit. Open to the right again, deflecting an additional *tsuki* with a rolling block. Touch your *kissaki* to her left wrist to complete *nagare kukuri makiuchi zuki sabaki.*

TAIJUTSU
Your partner grabs your right shoulder with her left hand and strikes *shomen uchi* with her right. Open to the right as you guide her striking hand downward with your right hand underneath and grab over her hand with your left. Open to the right again, breaking loose from her grab on your right shoulder by swinging your right arm outward with enough force to break her grip. Keeping a lock on her right wrist, turn and take one more step to throw.

Practice Points
While we do practice both *katadori* (shoulder grab) and *munedori* (chest grab), *katadori* is more widely used here in the United States. The reason is simple. There are many women practitioners in the US and most women do not appreciate being grabbed on the chest while practicing. There are two different scenarios for this technique. In the first, *uke* grabs *nage's* shoulder and follows with a *shomen uchi* strike. In the second, *uke* grabs *nage's* shoulder but raises his other hand to block a strike returned by *nage*. Each scenario has a different *kenjutsu* relationship.

Kenjutsu   *Taijutsu*

Kenjutsu

Taijutsu

Kenjutsu

Taijutsu

11. Ushiro ryotekubidori—Kote gaeshi ura
Behind-both-wrists grab—Wrist twist (behind)

STRUCTURE ○ ○ △

No initial *shinogi* movement, beginning directly with *nukidomen sabaki* to *nagare kukuri makiuchi zuki sabaki*.

KENJUTSU

As your partner swings up to strike *shomen uchi*, slide right foot forward with *nukidomen sabaki*. Face to face, enter as she *tsukis*, blocking from the left as you both *tenkan* again. Face to face again, open to the right, deflecting an additional *tsuki* with a rolling block. Touch your *kissaki* to her left wrist to complete *nagare kukuri makiuchi zuki sabaki*.

TATEKI NO KURAI

Both partners swing up to strike *shomen uchi*. Slide across in front of your first partner with *nukidomen sabaki*. After your first partner *tenkans*, enter as she *tsukis* and both of you *tenkan* again. Open to the right, deflecting an additional *tsuki* from your first partner. Touch your *kissaki* to her left wrist to complete *nagare kukuri makiuchi zuki sabaki*.

TAIJUTSU

Your partner grabs both wrists from behind. Offer your left hand and *tenkan* under your partner's left arm. Grab over your partner's right wrist and *tenkan* again. Open to the right and take one more step to throw.

Kenjutsu	*Tateki no kurai*	*Taijutsu*

Kenjutsu, continued   *Tateki no kurai, continued*   *Taijutsu, continued*

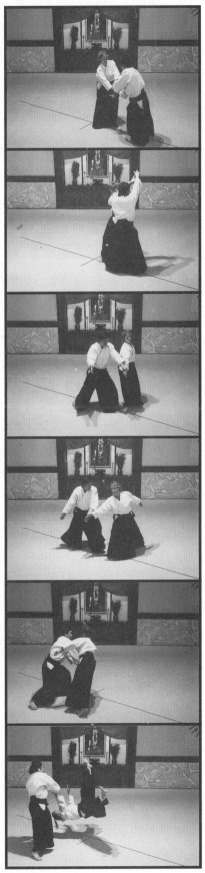

Kenjutsu, continued

Tsuka Sabaki
Sword Hilt Techniques

Many of the *katame waza* (joint stimulation techniques) practiced in Aikido can be found in other traditional Japanese martial arts, especially in schools of swordsmanship. *Koshi Mawari no Yojin* is a term used in schools of swordsmanship which translates as "to take care of one's waist area, or center." A sword is worn at the waist, and there are certain manners and etiquette associated with wearing a sword properly. There are also many techniques that have been developed to protect a sword from being taken while being worn. For example, if an enemy were to approach a samurai from behind and try to remove his sword by pulling backward, he would end up holding an empty case. The *tsuba* would keep the entire sword from slipping through the belt it was secured by. However, since the blade would be exposed with the cutting edge upward, were the enemy to push down on the handle of the sword, the blade would cut through the samurai's belt. This would not only release the sword, it would unbind the samurai's kimono, leaving not only an unprotected samurai but an undressed one! In this chapter, technique descriptions are given for instances when only a long sword is worn. The techniques vary if one is wearing a long and a short sword together.

There are many ways for someone to try to take a sword while it is being worn. An enemy can approach from the front, or behind, from the side, or even more than one at a time. This chapter illustrates techniques that counter a single partner approaching to take your sword from the front. These techniques utilize many wrist stimulations and should be practiced in the presence of an experienced instructor.

Kote Mawashi/Nikyo
Second Wrist Stimulation

1. Gyaku hanmi tsukadori— Soto kote mawashi (Nikyo)
Opposite-stance sword hilt grab—Outside wrist wrap (Second wrist stimulation)

KENJUTSU

Your partner grabs the *tsuka* (sword hilt) of your *ken* with his right hand. Move out to the left, securing his grasp on your *ken* by clasping your right hand over his. Rotate the *tsuka* to the left, clockwise, over the top of his wrist. Bow forward with *nikyo*.

TAIJUTSU

As your partner grabs your left hand palm down with his right, move out to the left, securing his grip on your hand by grabbing over his hand so that he cannot let go. Rotate your left hand in a circle, clockwise to the left and up over his wrist. With your left hand pointed toward his center, resting on top of his wrist, bow forward with *nikyo*. If you use your left shoulder as a support the stimulation is more powerful.

Kenjutsu

Taijutsu

2. Aihanmi tsukadori— Uchi kote mawashi (Nikyo) Same-stance sword hilt grab—Inside wrist wrap (Second wrist stimulation)

KENJUTSU

Your partner grabs your *tsuka* with his left hand. Move out to the right, securing his grasp on your *ken* by capturing his fingers with either hand. Rotate the *tsuka* to the right, counter-clockwise and up over the top of his wrist. Bow forward with *nikyo*.

TAIJUTSU

Your partner grabs your left hand palm down with his left. Move out to the right, securing his grip on your hand by grabbing over his hand with your right. Rotate your left hand in a circle to the right, counter-clockwise and up over his wrist. With your left hand pointed toward his center, resting on top of his wrist, bow forward with *nikyo*.

Kenjutsu

Taijutsu

3. Ryotemochi tsukadori—Uchi kote mawashi (Nikyo)
Both-hands sword hilt grab—Inside wrist wrap (Second wrist stimulation)

Kenjutsu

Taijutsu

KENJUTSU

As your partner approaches to grab your *tsuka*, draw your *ken* out slightly with both hands. As he grabs, move out to the right, trapping his hands with yours. Rotate the *tsuka* to the right, counter-clockwise, up over the top of his wrist. Bow forward with *nikyo*.

TAIJUTSU

Your partner grabs your left hand, palm down, with both his hands. Move out to the right, securing his grip on your hand by grabbing over his left hand with your right. Rotate your left hand in a circle to the right, counter-clockwise, up over his wrist. With your left hand resting on top of his wrist, bow forward with *nikyo*. As you apply the stimulation, your left hand should not grab your partner's wrist tightly. Extend your hand and push toward his center.

4. *Ryotemochi tsukadori—Soto kote mawashi (Nikyo)* Both-hands sword hilt grab—Outside wrist wrap (Second wrist stimulation)

KENJUTSU

Grab your *tsuba* with both hands as your partner grabs the *tsuka* of your *ken*. Move out to the left and rotate the *tsuba* in a circle, clockwise to the left. Place the *tsuka* on top of your partner's right wrist and bow forward with *nikyo*.

TAIJUTSU

As your partner grabs your left hand palm down with both hands, lead him by moving out to the left. Trap his right hand with your left as you move your hand in a circle clockwise to the left. With your left hand pointed toward his center, resting on top of his wrist, bow forward with *nikyo*.

Kenjutsu

Taijutsu

Kote Hineri/Sankyo
Third Wrist Stimulation

1. *Ai hanmi tsukadori—Kote hineri (Sankyo)* Same-stance sword hilt grab—Hand twist (Third wrist stimulation)

KENJUTSU

Hold your *tsuka* with your left hand, as your partner grabs your *tsuba* with his left. Anchor his hand to your *tsuka* with your right hand. *Tenkan* under his left arm and push inward with your *ken* with *kote hineri*. To avoid having your *ken* get lodged between you as you *tenkan*, draw it outward from your belt so that you can hold it at an angle more parallel to your body as you turn.

TAIJUTSU

As your partner grabs your left hand with his, trap his hand with your right over his hand and *tenkan* under his arm. Twist up with *sankyo*.

Kenjutsu

Taijutsu

2. Gyaku hanmi tsukadori— Kote hineri (Sankyo) Opposite-stance sword hilt grab—Hand twist (Third wrist stimulation)

KENJUTSU

Hold your *tsuba* with your left hand as your partner grabs your *tsuka* with his right. Anchor his hand to your *tsuka* with your right hand. *Tenkan* under your partner's right arm and push inward with your *ken* with *kote hineri*.

TAIJUTSU

As your partner grabs your left hand with his right, trap his hand with your right hand over his and *tenkan* under his right arm. Twist up with *sankyo*.

Kenjutsu

Taijutsu

Kote gaeshi/Wrist Twist

Gyaku hanmi tsukadori— Kote gaeshi
Opposite-stance sword hilt grab—Wrist twist

KENJUTSU

Hold your *tsuba* with your left hand as your partner grabs your *tsuka* with his right. Trap his hand with your right hand from underneath. Rotate the *tsuka* in a circle counter-clockwise to the left over your partner's wrist. Apply pressure to his wrist with the *tsuka* with *kote gaeshi*.

TAIJUTSU

Take your partner's balance by extending him forward as he grabs your left hand, palm down with his right. Rotate your hand in a circle, counter-clockwise over his wrist, and release your hand from his grasp by grabbing his hand from underneath. Open to the right, and twist his wrist to throw with *kote gaeshi*.

Kenjutsu

Taijutsu

Shihonage/Four-Direction Throw

Gyaku hanmi tsukadori—Shihonage
Opposite-stance sword hilt grab—Four-direction throw

KENJUTSU

Hold your *tsuba* with your left hand as your partner grabs your *tsuka* with his right. Rotate the *tsuka* over his wrist counter-clockwise to break his grip, and grab his right wrist with your right hand. Slide in front of your partner, right foot forward, extending your partner's arm in front of you. Step and pivot under his arm with *shihonage*.

TAIJUTSU

As your partner grabs your left hand with his right, cut a tight circle with your left hand, palm toward your partner, counter-clockwise over his wrist. Grab his hand from the left with your left hand and with your right hand as well. Extend your partner's arm in front of you as you slide across in front of your partner, right foot forward, step, and pivot to throw.

Kenjutsu

Taijutsu

Aikinage/Aiki Throw

Katatemochi tsukadori—Aikinage
One hand and sword hilt grab—Aiki throw

KENJUTSU

Your partner grabs your *tsuka* with his right hand and your right hand with his left. Hold the *tsuba* with your left hand and rotate the *tsuka* in a circle to the left clockwise over his wrist to loosen his grip. At the same time, raise your right hand upward, and slide, right foot forward under his left arm, step and pivot. Your partner is forced to let go of your *tsuka* as you pivot because the position becomes too painful to hold on. Keep a tight grab on your *tsuba* to avoid losing your *ken*, and extend your right arm to throw.

TAIJUTSU

As your partner grabs both your hands, cut a tight circle with your left hand, palm up, clockwise over his right wrist. Raise your right hand and slide, right foot forward, under his left arm, step and pivot. As you slide, trap your partner's right hand between your left hand and your left hip (as if you were holding the *tsuba* while wearing your *ken*). After you pivot, extend your right arm to throw.

Kenjutsu

Taijutsu

Batto Tachiai
Sword Unsheathing and Single-Cut Techniques

Batto tachiai are techniques used when an attacker approaches and you have not yet drawn your sword. *Shinogi* and *sabaki* movements are also clearly distinguishable in this group of techniques. Moving off the line constitutes your *shinogi* movement. Drawing your sword can be considered a *sabaki* movement used to deal with a second strike. *Batto tachiai* are advanced-level techniques, and many techniques fall into this category. This chapter illustrates a few of the most popular examples.

Shihonage
Four-Direction Throw

1. *Gyaku hanmi katatedori*—*Shihonage omote*
Opposite-hand grab—Four-direction throw (front)

KENJUTSU

As your partner swings up to strike *shomen uchi,* move out to the left. As he strikes downward, bring your weight down and bend your knees, dropping into a sword-drawing position. (See photo 4 in the *kenjutsu* series.) As your partner swings up again for his second strike, draw your *ken* and slide across in front of your partner, right foot forward. Time the draw to be able to cut across to his right armpit as he swings up to strike. Step, pivot, and strike downward in the opposite direction to complete *nukidomen sabaki.*

TAIJUTSU

As your partner approaches to grab your left hand with his right, move out to the left. As he grabs, cut a tight circle with your left hand, counter-clockwise, over his wrist with your palm facing toward your partner. Grab his hand from the left. Use the outside of your forearm to apply pressure under his elbow as you extend his arm in front of you with both hands. Slide, right foot forward, across in front of him. Step, pivot, and cut downward with your hands to throw.

Kenjutsu

Taijutsu

Kenjutsu, continued

Taijutsu, continued

2. *Aihanmi katatedori—Shihonage omote*
Same-hand grab—Four-direction throw (front)

KENJUTSU

As your partner strikes *shomen uchi,* open to the right into a drawing position. As he swings up for a second strike, match his timing, draw, and cut under his left armpit with your *kissaki,* right foot forward. Step and pivot, striking downward in the opposite direction to complete *nukidomen sabaki.*

TAIJUTSU

Your partner approaches to grab your left hand with his right. Extend your hand toward him, palm down, as he grabs and open to the right. As you open, take your partner's balance, tipping him forward past his center, and extend his arm in front of you with both hands. Slide across in front of your partner, right foot forward. Step, pivot, and cut downward with your hands to throw.

Kenjutsu   *Taijutsu*

Kenjutsu, continued   *Taijutsu, continued*

Iriminage
Entering throw

Tsuki—Iriminage
Punch—Entering throw

KENJUTSU

As your partner *tsukis*, open to the right into a drawing position. As he swings up again to strike *shomen uchi*, match his timing and draw your *ken*. Enter right foot forward and cut forward to his right wrist. *Tenkan* to the left, avoiding a strike to your right leg. Your partner also *tenkans* to regain position. Face to face, as your partner swings up again, match his movement. As he strikes downward, open to the right and strike *shomen uchi* to complete *nagare kukuri menuchi sabaki*.

TAIJUTSU

As your partner punches with his right hand, open to the right and hit down over his striking arm with the blade of your right hand. After your initial strike, grab over his hand and extend him forward slightly to take his balance. As he attempts to right himself, raise his arm upward in an arc clockwise and slide in right foot forward. *Tenkan* to the left, guiding your partner with a firm grasp of his neck or shoulder with your left hand. Take one more step forward with your right foot and enter with your whole body to throw.

Kenjutsu   *Taijutsu*

Kenjutsu, continued   *Taijutsu, continued*